W9-ATR-365

THE
PARADOX
OF
CONTROL

PAROLE SUPERVISION OF YOUTHFUL OFFENDERS

Patrick G. Jackson

PRAEGER

PRAEGER SPECIAL STUDIES • PRAEGER SCIENTIFIC

Library of Congress Cataloging in Publication Data

Jackson, Patrick G.
    The paradox of control.

    Bibliography: p.
    Includes index.
    1. Juvenile corrections—California. 2. Parole—California.
3. Parole officers—California. 4. Social Control. I. Title.
HV9105.C2J32 1983   364.6'2'088055   83-9516
ISBN 0-03-063524-1

Published in 1983 by Praeger Publishers
CBS Educational and Professional Publishing
A Division of CBS, Inc.
521 Fifth Avenue, New York, New York 10175 U.S.A.

© 1983 by Praeger Publishers

All rights reserved

23456789   052   987654321

Printed in the United States of America on acid-free paper.

364.62
J13

84-1236

Do not badmouth thyself, others or the Department.
Board member, orientation meeting, 1977;
a verbal addendum to the C.Y.A. Mission statement

I had to do it, my old lady is pregnant, I don't have any
money and man I got all these bills.
Parolee charged with robbery

The corrections worker must continually keep in mind
that his clients are irresponsible and inadequate, and they
have spent tedious years developing mechanisms to
hide their inadequacies and failures....The easiest way for
a parolee to cover his path is to lie. It is remarkable the
yarns that the parolee can sometimes spin!
"Ploys Used by Parolees," pp. 60-61 in Evrard,
Successful Parole. C.W. Thomas, 1971

The solution to the problem changes the nature of the
problem.
Peer's Law

Malinow's most important project once he gets out of
prison on parole is to get himself off parole.
"Annals of Crime, Part III," by Susan Sheehan.
The New Yorker, November, 1977, p. 200

Acknowledgments

I am deeply indebted to the California Youth Authority research staff, particularly Keith Griffiths and Elaine Duxbury. Along with Carolyn Davis, Jim Turner, Joe Seckel, and Carl Jesness, they provided an education in the everyday activity of California Youth Authority research and made my stay there as a graduate student assistant a fulfilling experience.

Keith Griffiths provided access to the study and the cooperation and support necessary for a fellowship to conduct it. No holds were placed on my research activities. Keith Griffiths and other staff offered constructive criticisms through their reactions to a rough preliminary draft of the study results.

William C. (Bill) McCord conceived and developed the Differential Status Project, which provided the basic data used in the present study. Bill McCord played a leading role in the project until it unexpectedly came to a halt in 1976. I hope I have adequately acknowledged his role in the project in this book. Bill McCord also introduced me to the Oakland superior and municipal court record-keeping systems and took much time and effort to provide materials related to the history of the project.

George Davis, former head of Information Systems, Max Zeigler, and Rich David gracefully provided all data requested. I wish to thank them all.

The views expressed in this study do not necessarily represent those of the California Youth Authority. Responsibility for the analysis and interpretations rests with me.

The material in this project was prepared under Grant 78-NI-AX-0029 from the Law Enforcement Assistance Administration, U.S. Department of Justice. Researchers undertaking such projects under government sponsorship are encouraged to express freely their professional judgment. Therefore, points of view or opinions stated in this document do not necessarily represent the official position or policy of the U.S. Department of Justice.

Floyd Feeney sponsored the grant proposal and kindly provided a quiet office to work in the Center on Administration of Criminal Justice. He also helped to develop an agreement with the Youth Authority to bring all research materials to the Center at the University of California, Davis campus and helped in countless other ways to make the research process easier. His support, organizational skills, and encouragement have been greatly appreciated.

The late Forrest (Woody) Dill was a constant critic and source of new ideas and prompted me to push forward and publish the study. Edwin M. Lemert, chair of the dissertation committee, encouraged my exploration of new ideas. I wish to thank him for his patience and guidance during the course of the study.

Sheldon Messinger, John Berecochea, and Deborah Star were very helpful in the beginning stages of the research. Dorothy Jaman provided data from the Department of Corrections. I owe a hearty thanks to Jim Cramer, Guy Pasela, and David Rudisill, who provided assistance with statistical problems. None of these individuals, however, is responsible for any mistakes.

Chris Zambrano, Robert Tillman, and Steven Story coded and collated statistics; their diligence and conscientiousness went far to erode stereotypes of of hired hand researchers. Connie Larson speedily typed three chapters of the text and helped in many other ways. John Sutton made useful editorial comments and helped type the remaining manuscript. Cindy Stearns helped to edit the final manuscript. I want to take this opportunity to thank them.

Contents

List of Tables and Figures

TABLES

FIGURES

1
Parole and
Social Control

Parole is currently in a state of crisis. The basic issue is whether parole as practiced today is an efficacious way of reintegrating offenders into the community (Studt, 1967). Recent investigators claim it is not, and call for its abolition.[1] Others claim that it is an effective deterrent or rehabilitation device and point out unforeseen and undesirable consequences of abolition.[2] Some argue that parole should be changed in such a way that it is given to parolees on a voluntary basis (Rubin, 1979).

The highly polemical controversy surrounding the question of parole today is in no small part a result of a failure to distinguish parole release and parole supervision. Parole as a method of release from prison is inseparable from the indeterminate or indefinite sentence. Parole release provides a means of control over inmate behavior or morale as well as the size of prison and parole populations. However, the traditional rationale for the practice is individualized rehabilitation tailored to fit the needs of the individual offender. Under ideal circumstances the parole board is able to identify the optimum time for release or "parole readiness" of prisoners—the point when further incarceration will do more harm than good and when the potential for a successful parole experience is at its peak.

Supervision after release, which is a primary concern of this study, is also closely tied to the indeterminate sentence. The parole board imposes special rules on the parolee during supervision in the community. The parole agent in theory provides services to aid rehabilitation as well as surveillance over the parolee for the protection of society. The parolee reports regularly to the agent and the latter makes unannounced visits at work or home. One result of this can be agent-recommended "revocation" of parole—that is, reimprisonment—

but on a variety of grounds other than law-breaking and conviction of a crime. Thus parole release and community supervision are closely related. The ubiquitous threat of reimprisonment which they represent is the primary basis for the widely held assumption that parole is a deterrent (Stanley, 1976; cf. Sacks and Logan, 1979).

Parole supervision may be understood as an example of the more general phenomenon of social control. Social control as defined here refers to formal and informal means of resolving disputes, conflicts, or potential or actual rule breaking. Passive or informal social control refers to internalized norms which inhibit the commission of deviant acts or to actions or accommodations which normalize and effectively inhibit such actions through their containment. Active social control refers to the means used by societal agents to control, manage, or suppress deviance.[3] In the present study active social control is usually accompanied by special rules (conditions of parole) for the offender which do not apply to free citizens.

The use of parole, both as a method of release from prison and as a means of control in the community, is grounded in the assumption that control over liberty and hence the motivation to freedom is an indispensable means for controlling, directing, or channeling parolee conduct. The use of community supervision to return parolees to prison, to temporarily detain or merely to use the threat of revocation as a means of protecting society makes parole a mechanism of social control. In the terms of this study, then, the question today is whether active social control as represented by parole supervision reduces crime.

PRIOR RESEARCH

Previous research does not present a clear answer to this question. In general, nonexperimental studies relevant to the question have found that parole supervision may reduce recidivism, while controlled, experimental studies find no effects. There are four categories of research related to this question: studies of the effects of reduced caseload size, of vastly reduced or zero-level supervision, of discharge from prison or jail compared to parole from either of these, and of early discharge from parole supervision.

Caseload Size

The number of studies and reviews of studies investigating the effects of caseload size on recidivism boggles the mind.[4] Nevertheless, research has not demonstrated that smaller caseloads reduce recidivism. In one study, smaller, "ideal" caseloads in the federal probation system were found to be associated with a higher percentage of technical violations than a large caseload group under regular supervision (Robison et al., 1969). Nonetheless, these studies have limited relevance to the present study because they have included some form of direct supervision and not a lack of supervision.

Outright Release from Prison or Jail

The second and most widely cited line of research is that which compares parolees and individuals discharged from prison for some reason other than parole, such as expiration of sentence (Waller, 1974; Zuckerman, Barron, and Whittier, 1953; Heaton and Adams, 1969) or because of a court order (Sacks and Logan, 1979). Lerner (1977) compares jail releases to parole or discharge and finds evidence favoring parole supervision. All of these studies are quasi-experimental; that is, they lack random assignment to parole or no parole.

It is difficult to interpret the findings of these studies in part because of a lack of controls over biases due to what Cook and Campbell (1979) have referred to as "selection" (cf. Moseley, 1977). In these studies bias due to selection may provide an advantage to parolees in terms of risk of failure. As Zuckerman, Barron, and Whittier (1953) stated in an early study of this kind, ". . . the parolees who figured in the current study . . . represent fairly select groups of 'better risk' for adjustment in the community." With the exceptions of Waller (1974), Gottfredson, Mitchell, and Flanagan (1982), and Lerner (1977), the studies comparing parolees and other releases from prison do not even so much as attempt to control for bias due to selection (Zuckerman, Barron, and Whittier, 1953; Heaton and Adams, 1969; Zumbrun and Berry, 1958; Department of Offender Rehabilitation, 1977).

One of the most recent studies using a nonrandom design, Sacks and Logan's, *Does Parole Make a Difference?* (1979), illustrates the problem of selection. The study compares the outcomes for 112 minor felony adult offenders released from prison due to a court decision with those of 57 offenders on parole who had been committed to prison for the same class of offense. The latter group had been on parole at least six months. They had also been released to parole approximately one year earlier than those discharged from prison. The results of this study show the parolees performing significantly better than the discharges as measured by the percentage convicted within one year. The study shows that 63 percent of the parolees and 39 percent of the discharges were conviction-free. No other major follow-up measure showed a significant difference. They did find that "low risk" subjects, as measured by number of prior nonprison sentences, did equally well while high risk discharges did worse than their counterparts.

Does this show that parole supervision accounts for the better performance of parolees? There is room for suspicion. The design of the study was "loaded" in terms of risk of failure for the discharges or selection bias. The discharges had more serious records, and one would expect them to have performed more poorly than those paroled. They had more prior sentences, a higher percentage had a history of alcohol abuse, the discharges were younger and were given sentences that were significantly longer than those of the parolees. The authors attempted to control for the differential risk of the two groups through use of more powerful statistical techniques. It is possible, though, that the two groups may differ on characteristics that were unmeasured and uncontrolled.

The parolees in the study, as noted earlier, had all been on parole for six months or more, while the discharges were new releases from institutions. Why were the parolees with less than six months of parole excluded? The authors explain in a revealing footnote: "The [Parole] Department advises us that it needs at least a six-month period in working with a parolee. We decided that it would make no sense to test the effects of parole on offenders with shorter periods of parole than that" (p. 7).

What the authors ignore is that exclusion of those with six or fewer months of parole eliminated a pool of potential failures. The authors' exclusion of these cases preempted the theoretically important comparison between discharges and individuals *newly* released to parole. To correct the methodological ingenuity here, one would have to exclude discharges in this study who had spent less than six months in the community, presumably before they were convicted of an offense, or revoked, which would have led to a termination of parole had they been placed on parole.

This study, like others with similar designs, compares the worse risks (discharges) with the best risks (parolees), finds differences favoring the latter and attributes them to the beneficial effects of parole supervision. This is not a test of parole but of the effects of selection—including selection by the parole board and the researchers. It is unclear whether use of more powerful statistical techniques in this study could or did control for unmeasured preexisting differences favoring the parolees.

More recently Gottfredson, Mitchell, and Flanagan (1982) examined the influence of parole on recidivism using a quasi-experimental design that compares outcomes of three categories of releases from adult prison: parolees, conditional releases, and inmates released at expiration of sentence without parole (called max-outs). These researchers used a more powerful statistical technique (logit analysis) to develop failure risk scores for individuals in each release category and then compared outcomes of the three groups within risk categories. "Failure" was defined in various ways but only one will be examined here: any new court commitment within five years of release from prison.[5] Based on the results of their analysis, the authors concluded that "offenders released on parole performed significantly better . . . both overall and in four of six risk groups, than either conditional releases or expiration of sentence cases."

Unfortunately their conclusion obscures more than it clarifies the results of the analysis for two reasons. First, "overall" comparisons (without controls for risk) defeat the primary purpose of the study, which was to use a more rigorous statistical method to control for unequal risk of failure between the parolees and discharges. Their results clearly show that the discharges are at greater risk of failure (1982, p. 294). Second, the method used to compare the outcomes of the three release groups did not adequately distinguish between the failure of the dischargees and the conditional releases relative to the better performance of the ordinary parolees. For my purposes the central question is how well the two categories of parolees performed relative to the discharges. But the statistical test of differences in failure, chi-square, was applied to the three groups simultaneously, masking important differences in performance.

In Table 1-1 I have shown the results of the overall statistical tests as reported by Gottfredson, Mitchell, and Flanagan (1982, p. 294) for each level of risk (Overall Outcome) and to the right of this the results of the chi-square test I computed for each specific group difference. In all cases where a significant difference exists it is in favor of the parolees and at the .05 level or below.

Table 1-1. Overall Statistical Test Results

Risk level of release	Overall Outcome[a]	Conditional Release vs. Parole	Conditional Release vs. Max-out	Parole vs. Max-out
1 (low)	sig.[b]	sig.	n.s.	sig.
2	sig.	sig.	n.s.	n.s.
3	sig.	sig.	n.s.	n.s.
4	n.s.	n.s.	n.s.	n.s.
5	sig.	sig.	n.s.	sig.
6 (high)	n.s.	n.s.	n.s.	n.s.

[a]As reported in M.R. Gofffredson, S.D. Mitchell, and T.J. Flanagan, "Another Look at the Effectiveness of Parole Supervision." *Journal of Research in Crime and Delinquency* 19: 277-298, 1982.
[b]sig., statistically significant at the .05 level or below, n.s., not statistically significant at the .05 level.

When the results are disaggregated in this manner the substantive interpretations of the study change. The conditional release parolees performed worse than the regular parolees in four risk levels (1, 2, 3, and 5), while the discharges performed worse in only two (1 and 5). However, the discharges and conditional releases did not differ in outcome at any risk level. Since the authors assert that conditional release is practically "indistinguishable" from ordinary parole one would expect both groups of parolees to perform similarly and both to perform better than the discharges. Neither argument is supported by their data. The fact that the ordinary parolees outperform the conditional parolees takes us instead to the paradoxical conclusion that *parole out-performs itself* and leads one to question how such a state of affairs could come about.

The key to this paradox most likely resides in the unmeasured and uncontrolled selection process by which offenders of differing risk levels become ordinary parolees, conditional releases, and max-outs. The unmeasured selection or "assignment" factors (Judd and Kenny, 1981) are most likely uncontrolled but related in important ways to the outcomes of the three groups and hence make attempts to separate treatment and selection effects extremely difficult. The use of more powerful statistical techniques for controlling measured prior differences between parolees and discharges in this study is certainly an advance in this area of parole research: when used correctly they can help to reduce bias.

Waller (1974, p. 199) also attempts to grapple with the issue of selection in a study with somewhat more similar pretest comparisons. He concluded that arrest outcome differences favoring parolees in his study of adult male felons disappeared when selection bias was controlled. Waller identified two potential sources of bias: that occurring among prisoners who applied for parole (and therefore selected themselves for parole) and the selection procedure of the board, which released individuals of lesser risk. He found that effects of the latter selection procedure were apparently overridden by the effects of inmate self-selection. In addition, he found that inmate perceptions of their ability to succeed on parole varied directly by their release status: direct discharges from prison felt more often that they would fail. In any event, the results of Waller's study, like those of Lerner (1977), and Gottfredson, Mitchell, and Flanagan (1982), which showed results favoring parole supervision, might still be biased because the analyses might not have controlled for preexisting differences between experimental groups that are related to outcomes.

A second difficulty with prior research of this kind has been stated by Star (1979, p. 15): ". . . parolees can be administratively returned to prison [i.e., via a technical violation and revocation of parole] in lieu of criminal prosecution—an option not available to discharges. This lack of equivalent criminal justice processing . . . could account for a lower court reconviction rate" and subsequent court return to prison for parolees. By the same token, it could account for a higher rate. This problem is probably not as serious today in some jurisdictions due to a decline in use of revocation. But in past studies return to prison for a technical violation is difficult to interpret because it is unknown whether such a violation would have resulted in court conviction. For example, in the study by Zuckerman, Barron, and Whittier (1953), recidivism outcome comparisons were made between 183 parolees released from prison in 1944-1945 and 110 individuals whose sentences had expired during this same period. All of the individuals were released from the Minnesota State Reformatory for Men and followed for at least five years. For outcome data the researchers relied upon FBI fingerprint registration reports, parole board files, police, and other sources. The results showed that 42 percent of the parolees and 47 percent of the expirees had no records; 33 percent of the parolees and 53 percent of the expirees had either a conviction for a felony or misdemeanor or a charge lacking a disposition; fully 25 percent of the parolees but none of the expirees had had their parole rescinded (Zuckerman, Barron, and Whittier, 1953, p. 625).

Based solely on court conviction data one might be led to conclude that the expirees performed "worse" than the parolees, assuming the charges that lacked dispositions were evenly distributed between the two groups. But this conclusion would not necessarily be justified since it is unknown whether the parolees who were revoked would have been convicted of a felony or misdemeanor had the parole board *not* revoked their parole. Going a step further, were one to base conclusions about outcomes on the percentage of individuals who had *no* contact with the criminal justice system (42 percent parolees and 47 percent expirees), one could also be in error in arguing that there is only a 5 percent difference between the two groups of releases. The reason for this is that the parolees may have been returned to prison for different offenses than the expirees because they were under active parole supervision. For these reasons a revocation in lieu of a court conviction is extremely difficult to interpret.

A third problem of such studies is that none clarify how much, if at all, individual differences among parole officers may contribute to inflating arrest rates of parolees. In Lerner's (1977) study, where arrest data were used as a follow-up measure, the parole officer's "invisible hand" provides a convenient explanation for research findings. The author assumes that parolees are more likely to be arrested because of their status; therefore, he reasons that arrests of the parolee are inflated measures of crime while those for discharges are conservative measures. These assumptions introduce considerable flexibility into interpretations of data—and indeed they can make anything but a one-sided interpretation of the effects of parole supervision impossible. Regardless of research findings the conclusions are obvious: 1. if discharges do worse, they *actually* have done worse than it appears; 2. if parolees do worse, it is because of supervisory inflation; and 3. if the two have similar outcomes the discharges may *actually* have done worse because of supervisory inflation. The author's foregone conclusion is not surprising; it is a fait accompli:

> The parolees have a greater risk of arrest due to the fact that they
> are under the surveillance of a law-enforcement officer . . .
> Obviously, the discharges are not subject to these potential threats
> of arrest. Nevertheless the parolees show a lower arrest rate, further
> strengthening the hypothesis that parole supervision reduces crim-
> inality (Lerner, 1977, p. 222).

The assumed effects of supervision are thus "strengthened" by the untested assumption that agents independently arrest parolees to such an extent that any observed differences may be explained with reference to this factor. What is missing in this study and most others is a measure of the *actual* extent of agent-instigated arrests of parolees. Without these data or knowledge about agent practices, it is unclear how to interpret findings.

Early Discharge from Parole

A third category of relevant research examines the effects of early discharge from parole. The best of these is Jaman, Bennett, and Berecochea (1974). The research assesses the effects of shortening the time span of parole supervision; that is, early release from supervision. This study is not directly concerned with the effects of differing caseload size, forms of supervision, or minimal supervision; it is concerned with the effects of absence of supervision.

Jaman, Bennett, and Berecochea (1974) compare the outcomes of 413 adult felons discharged from parole (due to an administrative order allowing this action) after *two* years of uninterrupted parole supervision, with 341 who were discharged from parole after *one* year with no incidents (police or parole agent arrests or absconding).[6] The results show no difference in outcome between the two groups. There were no differences in percent arrested or convicted, time to offense, or in the percent deemed criminally insane who received jail terms of over 90 days, a suspended prison sentence, or California Rehabilitation Clinic or prison commitments. These results offer suggestive evidence that parole stays may be shortened without a resulting increase in crime. In other words, shortening the length of social control may not increase crime. In this study it has no effect at all.

Reduced or No Supervision

Two experimental studies with random assignment and vastly reduced or no supervision have found no difference in outcomes for juveniles or youthful offenders (Hudson, 1972; Jackson, 1978). Hudson studied 234 male and female parolees selected from an original pool of 378 parolees. Exclusion of 38 percent of the cases from the original pool was due to parole board requirements for the study to proceed. It is unclear how these exclusions affected the composition of the study groups or their representativeness. Of those deemed eligible 120 were randomly assigned to minimal supervision and the remaining cases given regular parole supervision. The only two provisions of the parole contract for the experimentals were that they obey the laws of the community and notify their parole officer if they planned to move permanently from the community. The control group had regular parole supervision.

Follow-up after ten months showed that the experimentals had very little contact with their parole agents relative to the controls, apart from verifying that they did not have to see their parole officer. Using arrest and revocation data as outcome measures, Hudson found little or no difference in percent arrested, time to next offense, and time to parole revocation. Hudson did find, though, that significantly more control than experimental cases had their parole revoked during the follow-up. However, the offenses of the experimental boys which led to revocation were more serious than those of the controls (results for girls are discussed further below). It may be that only the more serious charges of the experimentals came to the attention of the parole board in this study. Overall, the results of the study suggest no difference between the experimental and control cases attributable to treatment effects.

Previously I conducted a limited and preliminary follow-up of 202 youthful offender parolees (included in the present study), 100 of whom were randomly and completely discharged from parole supervision and the remainder retained on regular parole supervision (Jackson, 1978). A 13-month follow-up of their record of arrests and convictions showed no difference between the groups in the relative percentage arrested, time to arrests, or severity of charges. Parolee charges, however, appeared to be more quickly disposed of in the justice system and were somewhat more likely to result in sentences to adult prison.[7]

Finally, Star (1979) recently studied the effects of a greatly reduced form of parole supervision called summary parole among adult felons in California. Summary parole, similar to Hudson's experimental condition of reduced supervision, required only one initial contact with a parole agent and a one year discharge review contact. This study used a "stratified" random assignment procedure in order to test a number of different hypotheses (interested readers are encouraged to examine the study for details). Of the 2,198 individuals processed for the study, 62 percent were excluded to satisfy agency criteria for the project to proceed. The remaining 835 cases were divided into high and low risk groups using their base expectancy scores, and then were randomly assigned to one of three groups: summary parole, regular parole, or a delayed placement pool. After their departure from institutions, 199 individuals were placed on regular parole and 201 on summary parole. These cases were then followed at 6 and 12 months duration.

The results of this rigorous study showed that the two groups experienced an approximately equal percentage of arrests and convictions, offenses of similar seriousness, and about the same custody-free time in the community and percentages returned to prison. However, the two groups were reincarcerated through somewhat different administrative avenues. After six months of exposure, approximately 33 percent of the summary parolees and 31 percent of the parolees under regular supervision who had contact with the criminal justice system were reimprisoned. Although 21 percent of the summary parolees were returned by the court and 11 percent by revocation of parole, only 9.5 percent of the regular parolees were returned by the court and the remaining 22 percent through parole revocation (Star, 1979).

THE PROBLEM

Parole research is burdened by one of two problems. Studies which find differences between parolees and nonparolees are methodologically questionable because they fail to control for selection bias. On the other hand, studies in which selection bias is controlled have tested variation only in the *amount* or *form* of parole supervision, not its presence or absence. Moreover, controlled studies find differences in reactions to individuals based on their parole status. It is significant, for example, that the studies by Hudson and Star found these differences in the processing of offenders rather than in treatment effects. Hudson found strong differences when controlling for sex: female parolees on minimal supervision received less lenient treatment than males, particularly for minor offenses. Moreover, both male and female controls in the study were more likely to have their parole revoked. When coupled with Star's findings, these studies indicate that as the experimental subjects' distance from the parole system increased (minimal supervision or contact), their likelihood of parole revocation decreased.

There is also some evidence for processing effects in my preliminary 1978 study. The California Youth Authority (C.Y.A.) parolees were more likely than those randomly discharged from parole to be sentenced to adult prison. One would expect the parolees to have been revoked and returned to the C.Y.A. rather than being sent to adult prison. This suggests that studies of parole effectiveness are flawed by not showing how extrajudicial factors, police, or other influences affect study findings. They also point to a more general weakness of many studies of correctional treatment: in these studies attention gets focused upon the problems of the individual offender and not upon the decisions and actions of officials who react to them.

Indications that differences in outcomes of treatment may reside in the activities of "treaters" or administrators rather than in "treatees" have been recognized in other studies. Lerman (1972), for example, has shown how recidivism outcomes favoring experimental cases in the Community Treatment Project may have been due to differential decision making about parole outcome. He argued that the nature of the discharge classification given to experimental and control cases differed when the two groups were charged with offenses similar in severity. High severity offenses of both groups had similar dispositions, but charges against experimentals of low and moderate severity led to more lenient discharge classifications than for control cases.

A review of the San Francisco Project (1965) by Adams, Chandler, and Neithercutt (1971, p. 50) suggests that the actions of officials may have caused a higher number of technical violations among individuals randomly assigned to intensive probation supervision than among those receiving regular probation supervision. Adams, Chandler, and Neithercutt note that the upsurge in technicals may have "resulted as expressions of defiance in response to the frequent authoritative intrusions into their lives."

Whether the rise in technical violations found in the San Francisco Project was due to probationer reaction to authority, a greater awareness of parolee status violations, or some other factor(s) is an important question. Whatever the source, it is clear that the research findings were at least in part an artifact of social control, what one may call *spurious recidivism*—recidivism which cannot be explained solely on grounds of probationer or parolee conduct. Spurious recidivism may develop at a variety of levels of the criminal justice process, including arrest, conviction, sentencing, and elsewhere.

In parole research spurious recidivism has been a problem of investigation in its own right, although it has not to my knowledge been defined in the terms used here. Specifically, some researchers have investigated the conditions under which parolees are likely to be revoked for technical violations of parole. For example, Dembo (1972) finds that parole officers whose orientation toward parolees is one of punishment and community protection are more likely to declare parolees in violation of technical rules of parole than officers whose orientation is one of offender rehabilitation and treatment. Battaglia (1968) relates decisions to revoke to attitudes of the officer as well as the visibility and seriousness of the alleged offense.

In one of the best field studies showing how precarious attempts to control parolees may produce spurious outcomes, Irwin (1970, p. 173) describes how these outcomes emanate from interaction between parolees and agents. He found that parole agents retrospectively reinterpreted the rules of parole upon indication of "trouble" on the part of the parolee. Previously tolerated parolee violation of the rules of parole were charged *ex post facto* against the parolee when agents recommended return to prison. This finding was later supported by Star and Berecochea (1977, p. 37), who find that when law violations are combined with status (technical) violations, there is a greater likelihood of parole revocation and return to prison.

Some researchers suggest that parole outcomes vary greatly according to regional or office differences in conceptions of conduct worthy of revocation. Decisions to file recommendations for revocation have been shown to vary by office. Much of the variation in recommendations could be explained by the attitudes of unit supervisors toward revocation (Robison and Takagi, 1970) or by "office culture" and the seriousness and visibility of parolee conduct (Battaglia, 1968). Robison and Takagi (1970) also found that office differences in recommendations to return to prison as determined by hypothetical cases (taken from actual files) were significantly correlated with actual returns to prison. In addition, the latter researchers found that differences between offices in recommendations for discharge from parole held when controlling for the "risk" level of parolees, as measured by base expectancy scores.

Finally, the Star, Berecochea, and Petrocchi (1978) study of board response to violation reports made by parole agents found that changes in revocation rates were not due to changes in parolee behavior but rather to changes in policies regarding revocation (cf Takagi, 1967).[8] They also found that actual parole revocation recommendation policies were largely shaped by the parole officers and not the parole board.

Based on past research it seems justified to conclude that the actions of officials must be taken into account when interpreting parole outcomes. Burkhart's (1976) summary of the results of the "Great California Parole Experiment" makes this point quite well. The article reviews a large number of innovative research projects in a state where parole practice is said to have reached its zenith of development. Spurious recidivism was an administrative fact of life in these studies, if not politically useful in the scramble for state monies:

> [T]he expansion of correctional research efforts in California was accompanied by growing evidence that parole outcomes, at least in terms of remaining in the community or returning to prison, were influenced more by system or policy changes than by specific treatment or supervisory efforts.

"The point," the author later writes, "is that major parole outcome findings can indeed be greatly affected by selective administrative actions" (1976, pp. 11-13).

The finding that parole outcomes may be a product of both parolee or probationer and official action reflects, in part, the wide discretionary powers parole and probation officers have held, at least in the past. Today it is unclear whether the discretion which served as a foundation for correctional field practices still exists in the same degree or form. Nor is it clear whether it was or is the same for adults and juveniles or youthful offenders. Some argue that parole has changed from what it once was (Sigler, 1975; O'Leary and Hanrahan, 1977), implying that studies conducted in the past may no longer be relevant.

The *Morrissey* and *Gagnon*[9] decisions, which came down in 1972 and 1973, support the view that change has occurred in parole and probation revocation hearings. The landmark *Morrissey* decision challenged the traditional right/privilege distinction in law and set forth a two-step revocation proceeding for parolees. The *Gagnon* decision, in turn, specified that attorney representation is permissible under some circumstances and extended the *Morrissey* ruling to probation revocations.

McCleary (1978, p. 20) has argued that *Morrissey* "had the same effect on parole agencies that *Miranda* has had on police departments." Above all else it has meant increasing bureaucratization of the parole function. Moreover, it has made the return of prisoners through revocation more costly than in the past, particularly in terms of time and effort required to justify revocation, development of necessary procedures, and their monetary outlay.

Viewed in this light it is unclear whether the field research conducted prior to *Morrissey* and subsequent administrative changes is still applicable today. Studt (1967, pp. 3-4) argued, for example, that parolees might be negatively affected by parole. She argues that parolees perceive the extremely costly consequences for failure on parole, a perception which increases over time: ". . . [F]or the parolee the constant jeopardy of return . . . means not only potential loss of liberty . . . but also further postponement or actual relinquishment of already over-due events in his life." And individuals "who are exposed to an unrelieved experience of high risk develop some sort of defensive adaptations [which] may assume the behavioral guise of either low commitment or habitual flirting with danger."

Irwin (1970, p. 173) finds the inconsistent, moralistic imposition of middle class values on parolees creates a sense of injustice:

> The [parole] agency, in attempting to pursue the two abstract and possibly conflicting goals of treatment and surveillance, and in attempting to impose, with great inconsistency, a conservative and moralistic behavior code on persons uncommitted to conventional values, has espoused a system to which the parolee must employ deceit and distance to adjust and in which the parolee remains in danger of being charged *et post facto* for acts which had been tolerated. This often produces or increases a sense of injustice and a further loss of commitment to conventional society.

In these studies the conclusion is almost inescapable that the parole function plays an important role in explaining why parolees do poorly on parole and that the revolving door from which so many find it difficult to escape is in part an artifact of the parole system. Many of the insights of these studies are undoubtedly still relevant today. Nevertheless, it may well be that the diminution— but not elimination—of revocation for technical violation of the rules of parole has altered the nature of correctional practices and hence the conclusions of the studies.

McCleary's (1978, p. 94) recent study of adult felon parolees in Illinois indicates that agents still maintain considerable discretion, albeit circumscribed by structural forces in the officer's environment. He finds that a parole officer "must decide which clients to save and which clients to sacrifice. This decision is determined to a great extent by personal considerations . . . and by organizations contexts." This study implies that officers do not have the unbridled discretion found in past studies (as far as returning prisoners for technical violations is concerned) and that their primary influence is in influencing court dispositions through participation in plea bargaining.

In this study, returns to the C.Y.A. for violations of technical rules of parole constitute only a minor percentage of the reasons for reinstitutionalization. This is congruent with a long-term decline in use of revocation for technical violations in the C.Y.A. The reduction of this practice helps to resolve some methodological and theoretical difficulties involved in interpreting the effects of active social control.

THE PRESENT STUDY

There is, then, a need for further research to correct for bias due to selection, test the effects of no supervision, understand differential reactions based upon a parole status under conditions of no supervision, and understand the extent of change in corrections related to revocation practices.

Many writers argue that parole as a means of release from prison is in drastic need of revision (Twentieth Century Task Fund, 1978; Foote, 1973). Others, however, argue that the proposal to abolish parole supervision is tantamount to "throw[ing] the baby out with the bath water" (Martinson and Wilks, 1977, p. 23). The question these authors raise is: "Would the abolition of the present system of parole supervision increase or decrease the rates at which persons released from incarceration would be reprocessed into the criminal justice system?" They correctly argue that previous research has studied the effects of variations of parole supervision, such as smaller versus larger caseloads, "within the existing system" of parole and is therefore of limited relevance to questions raised here.

What is needed, as stated by Stanley (1976, pp. 181-182) and referred to by Martinson and Wilks (1977) and Lerner (1977), is a study which permits a ". . . direct comparison of offenders under parole supervision with offenders set entirely free." Then the question can be properly asked: Does the imposition of active social control in the form of present parole practices reduce crime?

The present study addresses this question by examining the effects of random discharge from parole supervision as practiced in the C.Y.A., an agency for youthful offenders considered by some to be a leader in the treatment of offenders and to have high standards of parole supervision. The study randomly assigns individuals to either retention on or discharge from parole. The random assignment resolves many problems of past research. Most importantly, though, it allows a direct test of the effects of no parole supervision on recidivism and differential reactions based on a parole status in a controlled, experimental design.

Chapter 2 describes the study design, the representativeness of the study groups to the remaining C.Y.A. parole population, the meaning of discharge from parole and the data sources used in the 26-month follow-up.

Chapter 3 examines the arrest and conviction outcomes of the two groups. It also compares the nature of charges of the two groups and time to offenses. Chapter 4 looks at the extent to which parole officers and other criminal justice officials play a role in the arrest process of individuals.

Chapter 5 analyzes the sentencing outcomes of the two groups and attempts to understand the reasons for differential sanctioning.

Chapter 6 interprets the findings of Chapters 3 and 5. It places the results in the context of deterrence and labelling theory and provides interpretative materials for understanding sentencing differentials.

Chapter 7 briefly summarizes the results of the study and suggests that parole may reveal a paradox of control—that it either has no effects on crime or may even exacerbate the problem that it seeks to control.

NOTES

1. Citizen's Inquiry on Parole and Criminal Justice (1975); Fogel (1975); Stanley (1976); McGee (1974); Greenberg (1975).
2. See, for example, O'Leary (1975); O'Leary and Hanrahan (1977); Burkhart (1976); Sigler (1975).
3. The distinction between active and passive control is taken from Lemert (1972).
4. See Banks (1977) for a review of this literature, as well as Robison and Smith (1971), Waller (1972), and Greenberg (1977).
5. Gottfredson, Mitchell, and Flanagan state that this measure of failure "was the best approximation of a common criterion for the three release modes"; they note, however, that the approach "may have limited the time at risk for offenders under community supervision, and allowed technical violations in lieu of prosecution for a new offense to be counted as successes for supervised releasees."
6. Jaman et al. compared the two groups on 10 background characteristics and found no differences between them approaching statistical significance. It is possible that preexisting differences can explain the outcomes of the two groups, but the favorable comparisons of the proxy pretest measures suggest this threat to making inferences is lessened. Jaman et al. also followed a group discharged at expiration of sentence. These individuals were more likely to engage in criminal acts on a priori grounds, as they show in comparing their background characteristics with the other two groups discussed in the text. These max-outs also performed worse in the follow-up and are not discussed further here.
7. This study lacked complete information on arrest dispositions.
8. Takagi (1967) found that technical violation rates were reduced by administrative fiat. Parole officer promotions were to be judged in part on how greatly agents reduced the number of technical violations in their caseloads. This strategy, and others, was effective in reducing violations.
9. *Morrissey v. Brewer* 408 U.S. 471 (1972); *Gagnon v. Scarpelli* 411 U.S. 778 (1973).

2
Study Design, Comparability of Study Groups, the Meaning of Discharge from Parole, and Data Collection

The purpose of this chapter is to describe the study design, the reasons for exclusions from random assignment, compare the discharges and parolees on selected background characteristics, discuss the meaning of discharge from parole, and describe the methods for collecting follow-up data. The conclusion is that randomization produced comparable study groups. This means it is not likely that the comparisons of outcome data will be biased by a design which favors one group over the other on a priori grounds. Some comparisons are also made between the study groups and remaining parolees in the state as of December 31, 1975, on background characteristics and parole outcomes. These comparisons indicate the two groups are similar.

STUDY DESIGN

The area chosen for study is located in the East Bay area of California, and includes the Richmond, Hayward, and Oakland parole units. Eligibility criteria for inclusion in the study were developed and eventually applied to the parole cases in these units.[1] Altogether there were 725 parolees on active supervision.

The bulk of the exclusions were on "Full Board" or "On Violation" status; together they total 58 percent of the 411 exclusions from random assignment. The jurisdiction of another 18 percent was to expire by July 1, 1976, which would have left too short a period in which to assess the role of active supervision. The remainder of the exclusions were for cases pending transfer outside the study area (9 percent), "Special Service" cases and residence outside the study area (each 6 percent), out-of-state cases (3.6 percent), and those with no file available to make a determination (1 percent). Thus only 314 or 43 percent

Table 2-1. Population Losses

Study status	Total		Discharges		Parolees	
	No.	%	No.	%	No.	%
Total randomly assigned	314	100.0	104	100.0	210	100.0
Exclusions	18	5.7	6	5.8	12	5.7
No follow-up record available						
Record sealed	2	0.6	2	1.9	0	0.0
Record purged	1	0.3	1	1.0	0	0.0
Charges outstanding or in custody	12	3.8	3	2.9	9	4.3
Other[a]	3	0.6	0	0.0	3	1.4
Total less exclusions	296	94.3	98	94.2	198	94.3

[a]Three cases retained on parole were discharged prior to March 1, 1976.

of the 725 individuals were eventually assigned to either retention on or discharge from parole (see Appendix 1).

Of the 314 cases randomly assigned only 296 were eventually followed (see Table 2-1), and 6 percent of both the discharges and parolees was excluded. Most of the attrition occurring after the time of random assignment and before the actual starting date of March 1, 1976, was due to the fact that some individuals (12 total) were either placed in custody or had charges outstanding. This included 3 percent of the discharges and 4 percent of the parolees. The remaining exclusions were due to a sealed or purged follow-up record (3 cases) or because a parolee case was actually discharged from parole before the study began (3 cases). The 296 individuals were then followed for 26 months, from March 1, 1976, to April 30, 1978.

The possibility that attrition after randomization might have altered the characteristics of the two groups does not appear serious. To determine whether the two groups are equivalent, however, comparisons were made between the two groups on selected background characteristics.

Discharge and Parolee Comparisons

Table 2.2 compares the discharges and parolees on over 30 background characteristics. The chi-square tests of difference between the two groups on these items indicate no differences at the .05 level of significance. What follows is a brief summary of data contained in this table.

The study groups are largely male, black, juvenile court commitments with no history of parole violations or court recommitments for their most recent parole stay. There are small differences in prior record, with the discharges showing 10 percent more cases with local commitments and delinquent contacts. The discharges also show a slightly higher percentage of first commitments to the C.Y.A. This statistic refers to the individual's most recent commitment to the C.Y.A., and not to past commitments followed by a discharge from the C.Y.A. The discharges also show a somewhat higher percentage of cases with "high" base expectancy scores, one indicator of overall parole "risk" for large numbers of cases.

Most have never been married; 14 percent of both groups have one or more children. They are predominantly Protestant. Close to 20 percent of each group has escaped from institutions in the past, not including the C.Y.A. The parolees were only slightly more likely to have had a co-offender at the time of their commitment offense. At the time of initial appearance before the parole board between 86 percent and 90 percent of both groups were recommended for institutionalization; 6 percent and 10 percent were actually recommended for parole.

Between 46 percent and 52 percent of both groups had a weapon associated with their offense, but for a sizeable proportion there was no information.

Table 2-2. Selected Background Characteristics of Study Groups

Characteristic	Discharges		Parolees	
	No.	%	No.	%
Sex				
Male	91	92.9	184	92.9
Female	7	7.1	14	7.1
Race				
White	33	33.7	70	35.4
Black	54	55.1	111	56.1
Mexican-American/other	11	11.2	17	8.6
Prior record				
None	3	3.1	12	6.1
Delinquent contact only	31	31.6	76	38.4
Local commitment and contacts	39	39.8	58	29.3
Two or more commitments	25	25.5	52	26.3
Felony/misdemeanor status				
Juvenile	52	43.1	85	42.9
Adult misdemeanor	29	29.6	70	35.4
Adult felony	17	17.3	43	21.7
Admission status (current)				
First commitment	77	78.6	138	69.7
Recommitment	21	21.4	60	30.3
Parole violator	12	12.2	31	15.6
Court return	9	9.2	29	14.6
Parole violations[a]				
None	81	82.7	158	79.8
One	13	13.3	31	15.7
Two or more	4	4.1	9	4.5
Recommitments				
None	87	88.8	163	82.3
One	11	11.2	32	16.2
Two or more	0	0.0	3	1.5
Parole returns				
None	77	78.6	138	69.7
One	11	11.2	39	19.7
Two or more	10	10.2	21	10.6
Base expectancy score				
Females (none)	7	7.1	14	7.1
1 (low)	24	24.5	54	27.3
2	32	32.7	70	35.4
3	9	9.2	27	13.6
4	16	16.3	17	8.6
5 (high)	10	10.2	16	8.1

Characteristic	Discharges		Parolees	
	No.	%	No.	%
Marital status				
Unknown	3	3.1	5	2.5
Never married	90	91.8	178	89.9
Married	2	2.0	14	7.1
Divorced/separated	3	3.1	1	0.5
Number of children				
None	76	77.6	155	78.3
One or more	14	14.3	28	14.2
Unknown	8	8.2	15	7.8
County of commitment				
Alameda	61	62.2	125	63.1
Contra Costa	26	26.5	50	25.2
All others	11	11.2	23	11.6
Interpersonal Maturity Level score				
Unknown/missing	19	19.4	32	16.2
I-2	4	4.1	11	5.6
I-3	49	50.0	102	51.5
I-4	26	26.5	53	26.8
Full board status				
Never on	97	99.0	195	98.5
First time on	0	0.0	2	1.0
Off was on	1	1.0	1	0.5
Special service status				
Never on	97	99.0	191	96.5
First time on[b]	0	-	1	0.5
Off was on	1	1.0	6	3.0
Violation status				
On violation[b]	6	6.1	10	5.1
Not on violation	92	93.9	188	94.9
Religion				
Unknown	5	5.1	10	5.1
None	14	14.3	34	17.2
Catholic, Orthodox	28	28.6	43	21.7
Protestant	50	51.0	107	54.0
Jewish and other	1	1.0	4	2.0
Number of dependency contacts				
Unknown	1	1.0	2	1.0
None	85	86.7	172	86.9
One of more	12	12.2	24	12.1
Number of prior escapes				
Unknown	2	2.0	4	2.0
None	77	78.6	155	78.3
One	11	11.2	26	13.1
Two or more	8	8.2	13	6.6

Characteristic	Discharges		Parolees	
	No.	%	No.	%
Number of cooffenders				
None	57	58.2	98	49.5
One or more	40	40.8	98	49.5
Unknown	1	1.0	2	1.0
Staff recommendation at initial appearance				
Unknown	1	1.0	4	2.0
Regular parole	6	6.1	20	10.1
Parole special program	1	1.0	1	0.5
Institution no psychological treatment	88	89.8	170	85.9
Institution with psychological treatment	0	0.0	2	1.0
Other	2	2.0	1	0.5
Weapons associated with offense				
Unknown	28	28.6	56	28.3
Yes	45	45.9	103	52.0
No	25	25.5	39	19.7
Alcohol associated with offense				
Unknown	39	39.8	77	38.9
Yes	47	48.0	94	47.5
No	12	12.2	27	13.6
Parental marital status				
Unknown	4	4.1	4	2.0
Never married	10	10.2	19	9.6
Married	23	23.5	54	27.3
Divorced/separated	61	62.2	121	61.1
Location of parole unit				
Richmond	30	30.6	52	26.3
Hayward	34	34.7	67	34.0
Oakland	34	34.7	79	40.0
Commitment offense				
Robbery	17	17.3	40	20.2
Assault and battery	8	8.2	9	4.5
Burglary	24	24.5	62	31.3
Theft (not auto)	14	14.3	23	11.6
Auto theft	10	10.2	21	10.6
Sex	1	1.0	1	0.5
Narcotics/drugs	4	4.1	15	7.6
Escape	6	6.1	8	4.0
Incorrigible	2	2.0	5	2.5
Placement failure	3	3.1	6	3.0
Miscellaneous felony	4	4.1	0	0.0
Miscellaneous misdemeanor	5	5.1	8	4.0

Characteristic	Discharges		Parolees	
	No.	%	No.	%
Months prior parole as of 3/1/76:				
latest parole stay				
2-6 months	31	32.6	56	28.3
7-12 months	15	15.3	50	25.2
13-18 months	11	11.2	40	20.2
19-24 months	11	11.2	14	7.1
25-30 months	6	6.1	10	5.0
31-36 months	11	11.2	10	5.0
37-42 months	3	3.1	7	3.5
43-48 months	4	4.1	7	3.5
49-120 months	5	5.1	4	2.0
Mean	18.4		15.1	
Standard deviation	16.6		12.5	
Median	14.5		11.2	
Age as of 3/1/76				
17 and under	7	7.1	8	4.0
18	15	15.3	36	18.2
19	12	12.2	40	20.2
20	27	27.6	38	19.2
21	14	14.3	31	15.6
22	13	13.3	39	19.7
23	6	6.1	15	7.6
24	4	4.1	6	3.0
Mean	20.1		20.4	
Standard deviation	1.9		1.8	
Median	20.1		20.3	
Months from latest admission				
to parole				
5 months and under	13	13.3	27	13.6
6-8 months	30	30.6	61	30.8
9-12 months	33	33.7	67	33.8
13-15 months	14	14.3	24	12.1
16 months and over	8	8.2	19	9.6
Mean	9.7		9.8	
Standard deviation	4.6		5.2	
Median	9.5		9.1	
Months from 3/1/76 to				
jurisdiction termination				
12 months and under	21	21.4	33	16.7
13-24 months	25	25.5	56	28.3
25-36 months	27	27.6	67	33.8
37-48 months	19	19.4	28	14.1
49 months and over	6	6.1	14	7.1

Characteristic	Discharges		Parolees	
	No.	%	No.	%
Mean	26.9		26.8	
Standard deviation	14.8		13.3	
Median	26.0		26.1	
Months from first admission to 3/1/76				
12 and under months	8	8.2	17	8.5
13-18 months	15	15.3	33	16.6
19-24 months	17	17.3	30	15.1
25-30 months	11	11.2	22	11.1
31-36 months	11	11.2	20	10.6
37-42 months	9	9.2	11	5.5
43-48 months	6	6.1	13	6.5
49-54 months	4	4.1	12	6.0
55-60 months	5	5.1	13	6.5
61-66 months	4	4.1	5	2.5
67-72 months	3	3.1	8	4.0
73 and over	7	7.1	14	7.0
Mean	35.5		36.4	
Median	30.5		30.0	
Standard deviation	21.4		23.4	
Months from first admission to jurisdiction termination				
24-36 months	5	5.1	10	5.0
37-48 months	11	11.2	40	20.1
49-60 months	33	33.7	48	24.1
61-72 months	26	26.5	49	25.1
73-84 months	12	12.2	24	12.1
85-96 months	6	6.1	13	6.5
97 to 170	5	5.1	14	7.0
Mean	62.3		63.2	
Median	59.5		61.0	
Standard deviation	17.8		22.6	

[a]Most recent parole stay only.
[b]Off at the time of random assignment.

Although 48 percent of both groups had alcohol associated with their offense, again there is missing information. The overwhelming majority have broken homes, comprising 61 percent to 62 percent of the individuals. The commitment offenses of the two groups are generally similar. The discharges have a slightly higher percentage of assault and battery charges and miscellaneous felonies, and the parolees a greater percentage of burglary.

Overall, the two groups had spent a median of about 12 months on parole as of March 1, 1976, the starting date of the study. All had spent at least two months on parole. One had spent 120 months. The skewness of the distributions and large standard deviations make an ordinary t-test of means inappropriate. Instead, the distributions were divided at the overall median and a chi-square test performed on the 2 by 2 table. The difference is not significant.

Finally, the two groups have exactly the same mean age (20), served about the same mean number of months in institutions before their most recent parole, had approximately equal time remaining in jurisdiction of the C.Y.A. as of March 1, 1976 (mean = 27 months), spent approximately equal time under the jurisdiction of the C.Y.A. (institutions and parole time combined) as of March 1, 1976, and had about the same sentence lengths.

This check on the random assignment procedure indicates that the two experimental groups compare quite favorably on the items examined here. One might ask, in addition, whether the study groups are similar to the remaining parolees in the state on C.Y.A. parole at the time the study began. (These data can be found in Appendix 2.) Briefly, the comparisons indicate that the study groups differ in characteristics related to the exclusionary criteria. Perhaps because of this the study groups contain a somewhat higher percentage of individuals with property-related commitment offenses. The study groups also have a higher percentage of blacks, which reflects the racial composition of the study area. The comparisons also indicate that there are no differences in the actual parole follow-up outcomes of the 198 randomly assigned parolees and the remaining parolees in the state at 15, 24, and 48 month intervals. The data thus suggest the parolees in this study do not differ greatly from the remaining C.Y.A. population in ways strongly related to recidivism.

THE MEANING OF DISCHARGE FROM PAROLE

Late in the month of February 1976, the wards included in the discharge group received the letter appearing on the following page. Very few, if any, of the wards were forewarned of their inclusion in the project.[2] As far as I could determine none of those who were discharged complained in any written or oral form.[3] The only reason the wards were given for their discharge was that they were "selected for a study to see whether young people now on parole [can] do just as well on their own." They were also given a brief lecture: "We hope you will make good use of this opportunity to remain a free, law-abiding citizen, making your own decisions and responsible for your own actions."

February 9th 1976

Dear

Enclosed is a copy of the Youth Authority Board Order
granting you a General Discharge from parole effective
March 1st, 1976. A limited number of persons including
you have been selected for a study to see whether young
people now on parole could do just as well on their own.

We hope you will make good use of this opportunity to
remain a free, law-abiding citizen, making your own
decisions and responsible for your own actions. After
you have gone at least one year with no arrests; contact
Mr.   Youth Authority,   Avenue,
Richmond, California 94805, phone   , to change
your discharge classification from General to Honorable.

If you have more questions get in touch with your parole
agent before March 1st.

                    Very truly yours,

                    Allen F. Breed, Director

                    by:

                            Parole Agent

There is no information available from the exparolees on their reactions to receiving the letter. One parole officer stated that some of the youth in his case-load were "very happy" to be discharged. Probation officers who were required to summarize the life situation of discharges upon rearrest were not usually aware of the experimental status of the arrestee. The only cases I have seen where the experimental status of the wards came to light were those involving C.Y.A. wards who were discharged from parole after having been on it for less than four months and who got into "trouble." Insofar as official documents show, the remainder of the discharges were treated as if they had been discharged from the C.Y.A. in the "usual" manner. One probation officer who prepared a report explaining the case of a discharge who was returned to court for a burglary noted that:

> . . . what we have here is a young man who was paroled from the Youth Authority, given a ride home and told he was free to do as he pleased. He was a part of an experiment conducted by the Youth Authority some time ago. I can't believe this young man, with a record such as his, is in the community without supervision.[4]

A recent memoir of an exprisoner and parolee speaks to subjective aspects of discharge from parole:

> I was discharged. Finally free. Free to be lonely. Free to go broke. Free to fail. Free to deal with the still ominous mysteries of my own most intimate nature. Still I was free. Unless I went back to my old trade no one could lock me in handcuffs and carry me off to jail, and I couldn't imagine I'd ever steal again. (Braly, 1976, p. 369)

The frequent recognition by parole officers that their charges dislike being on parole is reflected in Sheehan's (1977, p. 200) succinct summary of a prisoner's plan: "Malinow's most important project once he gets out of prison on parole is to get himself off parole." The passage by Braly amplifies this by showing that the point of discharge from parole was a time at which he defined his life as his own—his fate unfettered by his parole status.

THE AGENTS AND PAROLEES

If there is any consensus in the Youth Authority, or in many parole agencies, when parole supervision is most necessary and/or beneficial, it is at the point of the offender's entry into the community, particularly during the first months after release.[5] The purposes of parole and the priorities to be followed in implementing them are found in the parole manual:

Under temporary restrictions for the community's protection, the offender receives guidance and supervision directed at reintegrating him into society. The primary aim of parole is to protect society by preventing, or reducing, the likelihood of further illegal behavior. The second objective is to help the parolee adjust satisfactorily to social norms and to discover ways that he can put his abilities to self-satisfying and socially-constructive uses.

In order to accomplish these objectives, the following order of priorities has been established for parole staff:

1. Provide surveillance to ensure that parolees observe all conditions of parole and report violations to the Youth Authority Board.
2. Ensure that parolees' constitutional rights are protected. They are to be treated in a fair, just, and humane manner and their rights shall be limited only to the extent absolutely necessary and rationally related to the protection of the public.
3. Serve as service brokers or resource managers in order to assist parolees in obtaining employment, adequate housing, financial assistance, social and medical services, and other resources or services needed for their rehabilitation.
4. Provide counseling and direct services to parolees as needed.
5. Develop and maintain community acceptance, understanding, and support.[6]

Parole agents are faced with a formidable task, one which increasingly appears close to impossible: they must keep their charges out of trouble, find them a job, provide counseling and assistance to involuntary "clients" wherein the agent plays both cop and counselor, mediate familial difficulties, help the parolee deal with the court system when trouble arises, and explain and enforce board policies on revocation, temporary detention, and urine testing. Many of their parolees live in the most depressed areas of the city with peers who may be involved in criminal activities. As seen earlier, most have broken homes, few are married, although others live in consensual unions. Most are unemployed, have few job skills, and haven't graduated from high school. Employers do not often hire young adults with criminal records, and those who do frequently offer only exploitative or dead-end jobs. Officers must rely upon the voluntary cooperation of other service agencies, a long-standing policy in the C.Y.A., in attempts to help parolees.[7]

For the parolee, this period is roughly what Irwin (1970, p. 107 and passim) describes as one of disorientation and "meeting the exigencies of civilian life," not greatly unlike the situation confronting returning prisoners of war. McArthur's (1974) study of this transitional period among boys paroled from a juvenile reformatory characterizes the move as one of "disorientation, estrangement, and alienation. The . . . major adjustment task from the boys [sic] standpoint is 'How do I fit in?' " (p. 44). Much of the distress is a result of inadequate feedback, reaction, and response to real life situations lacking in an institution; the world is confronted without anticipatory actions and reactions. Two-thirds of the boys he studied had difficulty sleeping, some perceived their homes as small at first, and that time appeared to pass very quickly. Others seemed "frightened and immobilized."

McArthur's findings go further, however, as shown in his argument that "the reentry experience is an increasingly negative one . . . things start bad and get worse." As evidence for this he shows that hedonistic activities are common directly after release, but that over time participation in these activities declines in frequency and importance. As one stated, "The novelty of being out is over." It is at this point that the parolees begin their journey as discharges in the present study, since all had been on parole for at least two months.

Both the discharges and parolees had letters sent by the C.Y.A. to the police and probation departments indicating that each ward was to be released on parole. From most indications by probation officers these memos were simply placed in a file of the ward if on probation or shredded if not. Police in some cases made a notation of the release in their kardex file.

The parolees, though, differed from the discharges during the follow-up period in important ways. The parolees with under three months of parole as of March 1, 1976, experienced approximately 5.7 contacts with their parole officer, excluding phone contacts. This amounts to an average of about 60 to 65 minutes per month of contact by month 4 or 5. For individuals on regular caseloads, which includes almost all of the present cases, the number of minutes of contact with the agent dropped to 40 to 45 by month 8, eventually decreasing to 25 minutes at month 21 and remaining fairly constant thereafter.[8]

Of course not all of these contacts simply relate to counseling, service, or surveillance. Each individual has an annual review. In addition, a high percentage of those eventually removed from parole for violations are removed during the first seven or so months on parole. During the time frame of the study, for example, 23 of the 65 individuals discharged during the first three quarters were for law violations resulting in discharge to adult prison, recommitment to the Youth Authority, discharge to probation or jail, or because of expiration of sentence while absconding. In other words, much time is devoted to satisfying board requirements relating to the violation process after parolees get into trouble.

Both the notification of the corrections community of the release status of the wards and the activities of agents may have important implications. Whether in fact the police watch parolees more closely than others is unclear (see Chapter 3). It is apparent, however, that parolees *perceive* that the police watch them closely. In a recent study conducted by the C.Y.A., fully 66 percent of those interviewed felt the police watched them closely.[9] One parolee in the present study told his parole officer: "Once the police know you, they're

going to keep picking you up anyway, so you might as well get into trouble."[10]
The perception appears more common among parolees who "failed" in the C.Y.A.
study (77 percent) than among the "successes" (54 percent).

Moreover, the postarrest helping and control activities of agents directed
toward parolees reflect parolee perceptions. For example, 57 percent of those
who "failed" in the C.Y.A. study viewed their parole agent as "always a cop" or
"usually a cop" and 31 percent felt the parole rules were "not at all" fair. In
contrast, a scant 2 percent of the "successes" felt their agents were usually or
always a cop and none felt the parole rules were "not at all" fair. Whether these
perceptions are a cause or effect of "success" or "failure" is an open question.
The fact that the discharges in the present study had no parole agent to contend
with during the follow-up cannot be set aside.

The remainder of this discussion describes the sources of information used
to collect the follow-up information. Further discussion of the follow-up information can be found in Chapter 5.

DATA SOURCES

The primary source of information on outcome was taken from criminal
"rap sheets." These documents are a central repository for criminal justice information in California, and are maintained by the Department of Justice,
Bureau of Criminal Identification and Information (C.I.I.). They contain information on an individual's birthdate, race, sex, weight, height, current probation
and parole status, time of expiration for a probation status, aliases, dates of
arrest, charge or charges, arresting agency, dispositions for charges and dates of
dispositions, outstanding warrants, and whether an individual has died. For individuals currently under the control of the Youth Authority or the Department
of Corrections, up-to-date information on their custody status is maintained
which may reflect parole revocations in lieu of prosecution or court-ordered
returns to a state or local facility.

The rap sheets do not contain information on pretrial detention or paroles
from county jail, nor do they report information on minor offenses such as driv-
ing without a license. All information posted on the rap sheet, however, is verified by a fingerprint from the arresting agency; if not verified a statement is
made to this effect on the rap sheet. Records of arrests sent to the agency are
supposed to be posted within 72 working hours.

The study primarily relies on data taken from official documents and therefore with crude measures of known criminal violations during the follow-up.
Much of the work done during the follow-up involved collecting information
missing from the rap sheets, largely dispositions. To have ignored the problem
of missing information and proceeded with the analysis would have raised more
questions than it would have answered. Fully half of all the individuals followed
had one or more instances of information missing from their rap sheets during

the study period. The lack of disposition information raised immediate problems of interpretation of outcome data. Could the lack of a disposition be construed to mean that the prosecutor decided not to file charges, that the case was dismissed at court, acquitted, or otherwise lacked a conviction? Could it be taken to mean that the individual had died, fled prosecution or that the case had simply not gone to court? Since some charges had not been cleared on the rap after 2 years of their appearance, it became clear, after some quick checks at court, that the information was not being posted on the rap for other reasons. A meeting with C.I.I. personnel verified the observation: as of August 1977, they were behind in posting over 90,000 documents onto rap sheets. Moreover, Alameda county was also slow in sending the needed information to C.I.I.

The use of rap sheets as a primary source of information was intended to minimize the likelihood of "stacking the deck" against the parolees because of the greater amount of "control" over and hence information collected on them. Relative to traditional outcome measures used in parole research—such as the nature of their discharge from the C.Y.A.—such an approach seemed both desirable and necessary since those discharged from parole could not be compared to the parolees on this measure. The traditional method has been criticized elsewhere (Lerman, 1972).[11]

It was necessary to use supplementary sources of information to clear dispositions which were unreported on the rap sheets: specifically, warrants, charges not filed in court, charges filed in court but with no disposition, and alternative dispositions—such as in one case where a sentence included an extension of probation and, upon the probation officer's recommendation and the individual's request, a fateful journey to Guyana, which was not reported on the rap.

Three additional sources of information were used during the study. The first came from C.Y.A. case files in the central office. These were used mostly for persons on parole during the follow-up period. Originally it was hoped to use these as one source for clearing dispositions unreported on rap sheets, but because they sometimes lacked crucial information,[12] their use was restricted to ascertaining whether the parolees experienced any recommitments during the follow-up period and the reasons for recommitment. This information was double checked at court (discussed below). The same information source was used for new commitments to the C.Y.A. for both experimental groups.

A complete movement history was obtained for each case included in the study from the time of original (most recent) commitment to the C.Y.A. until departure; in the case of new commitments (after discharge) a new movement record was obtained for this institution and parole stay. This included both discharges and parolees.

The second additional sources of information consisted of court and other local records (police, sheriff, and probation reports). These sources were used more often than any other to clear dispositions. Three county sheriff departments allowed access to their computerized retrieval system to resolve dispositions and several local police departments released information when court records could not be found. These cases usually involved charges never filed in court. There were few cases for which dispositions could not be located using these sources.

Third, the Department of Corrections allowed access to their records, clarifying ambiguities on the rap sheets as well as information on dates of parole and violation actions on parolees committed there. Checks were made for any adult prison commitments not reported on the rap sheets for both groups. Information for adult federal and out-of-state lockups were taken from the rap sheets.

Finally, rap sheets and other readily accessible documents do not provide information on time spent in custody awaiting trial or hearing. Between the time of the arrest and date of disposition, an individual could have been in jail or released on bail or promise to appear in own recognizance (OR) programs. Since rap sheets do not report systematic information on this the first assumption we would like to make is that pretrial detention and other time spent in jail or elsewhere is evenly distributed between the discharges and parolees. However, parole agents are required by the board to issue parole holds for parolees charged with serious offenses or who pose a "danger" either to themselves or others. Since field files were destroyed there is not direct information in the C.Y.A. on the extent to which holds were used by agents.

My attempt to collect detention data due to parole holds was thwarted by bureaucratic red tape when time was short. The only place where detentions due to holds are ordinarily found is on the booking form at the jail and often in field files. The latter were destroyed and arrangements were made with the jail keepers to collect this information at the jail. Upon my arrival the superintendent stated they did not have enough staff to accommodate me, contrary to a previous agreement, *and* that it would be necessary to receive permission from the Sheriff's Department, a process felt to be overly time consuming.[13]

The information gathered was recorded for all offenses logged on the rap sheets during the period beginning March 1, 1976, and ending April 30, 1978. Rap sheets were first reordered for cases missing information. Duplicate rap sheets were useful only for a small number of cases with recent charges. The remaining cases required additional fieldwork.

NOTES

1. The exclusion criteria were developed largely to satisfy board requirements for the project to proceed. Full board, special service cases, and individuals on Violation status were required to be excluded. See, "The Course of the Study," Appendix 3 for a discussion of the development of the study.

2. To my knowledge no individual retained on parole was notified of his or her experimental status, at least formally. For a narrative description of the study see "The Course of the Study," Appendix 3.

3. One discharged parolee contacted his former agent a year after the study began in order to have his discharge classification changed from a "General" to "Honorable." This was so he could take over a small business of his father's, which was apparently prohibited given the ward's discharge status. All of the discharged wards were granted a General discharge. The case mentioned reminded the study's original investigators that the discharged cases were supposed to have been evaluated for a possible upgrade, but not a downgrade, in their discharge classification. The upgrading task was largely undertaken by Bill McCord.

4. Taken from a presentence report written by a probation officer late in 1976. It should be clear that not all the discharged cases received such treatment. As shown in Chapter 2, the overall median number of months spent on parole before the discharges were discharged was 11.8 months.

5. The strong belief in this assumption is reflected in the parole reorganization which has taken place since this study. Intensive parole services in the reorganization plan are "front loaded" for the first few months in entirely separate units, after which the parolees are transferred to a different parole officer at another, long-term, unit.

6. *Parole Services Administrative Manual*, Section 500. California Youth Authority, 1976.

7. See Smith (1955, pp. 45-81) and Bolen (1972, pp. 159-174).

8. Computed from State of California Department of Finance, *California Youth Authority Parole Program Effectiveness*, Appendix F, p. 89, 1976 (October). The same figures, of course, apply to the discharges during the time they were on parole.

9. Unpublished data taken from the "Success on Parole" Project in the California Youth Authority. Quoted with permission from Mark Weideranders. The study randomly sampled wards and interviewed them while in institutions and after parole. "Failures" in the study were defined as revocations.

10. Taken from the ward's parole violation report, C.Y.A., 1977, located in the Central file system, Sacramento, California.

11. Note that Lerman does not criticize the use of rap sheets in the Community Treatment Project, and in fact uses them as baseline data to demonstrate differential reaction and decision making. I do not wish to imply that these rap sheets are "pure" data. The question here is whether the parole bureaucracy can significantly affect what gets posted on the rap sheet above and beyond their "impurities" which develop because of other system biases. The assumption here is that these "other system biases" are equal or near equal for both the parolees and discharges.

12. For example, one agent's report of a disposition for receiving stolen property was one year of probation. Inspection of the court record indicated that the first three months of probation was to be spent in jail. McCleary's (1978) sometimes humorous discussion of the manner in which agents use records to slant reports to the board is relevant here. He also notes in an earlier article that the acronym C.Y.A.—interpreted as Cover Your Ass—was perfected by C.Y.A. parole agents in its early period and continued to the present day. This general use of records in my opinion obviated their use for finding dispositions. The reports are useful for study in their own right, however.

13. To gain some first-hand knowledge about the use of holds and warrants I visited two parole units in the study area and spoke with two unit supervisors and six parole agents who worked in the area during the time frame of the study. Most felt that detainers were used when parolees were *already* held in custody with or without bail, that in cases where bail was set it was so high the parolee would not be able to make it anyway. In the words of one agent, but not all, "Detainers are a meaningless gesture. We do it to protect our ass [from the board]."

Use of detainers where the parolee was not held on bail was generally felt to be infrequent. (Recollections of the use of holds during the specific time period of the study were difficult; the general consensus, however, was that the situation had not changed very much. Thus the observations made below apply to present-day practices but generally reflect what happened in the recent past.) At least one reason for their infrequent use beyond that required by the board is found in some agents' statements to the effect that holds are detrimental to the parolee. One stated that he had had a parolee in jail for 13 months on a hold, for which he "caught hell" from the defense attorney (DA) but not the prosecutor, who didn't mind.

So detainers or holds in cases where the parolee would otherwise have been set free do occur. The *extent* of their use above that which may be imposed at court is uncertain, but it seems reasonable to assume that detainers did not result in an amount of "excess" custody time far greater than that of the discharges, especially since C.Y.A. detainers were not honored in Alameda County for an unknown period of time during the study period. Overall, the time in custody for both groups is undoubtedly higher than presented here.

3
Social
Control Specified:
Effects of Parole on
Arrest and Conviction

This chapter compares outcomes for those discharged with those paroled on a number of indicators of criminal behavior, including but not limited to arrest record, convictions, time spent in custody, nature of charges, and severity of offenses. These findings boil down to this: at the very least there is no evidence of treatment or supervision effects resulting in lowered recidivism; at most there is evidence that the parolees performed worse on various measures of outcome than the discharges.

OFFENDERS IN THE COMMUNITY

One question which arises when discussing the efficacy of the parole system is whether the presence or absence of parole supervision or a parole status reduces or prevents criminal behavior. Were parole supervision such an agent, one would expect the discharges to be arrested more often, to commit offenses sooner, to be convicted for more offenses, to spend more time in custody—in short, to be less law abiding than the parolees.

Given the fact of random assignment and the demonstrated similarity of the two groups, we may more confidently assume that differences or similarities in outcome are not necessarily a result of selection bias.

How Many Are Rearrested?

In both the parole and discharge groups, 86 percent had at least one entry posted on their rap sheets during the 26-month follow-up period, as shown in

Table 3-1. This includes 87 percent of the discharges and 85 percent of the parolees. These data include minor offenses, warrants with outstanding dispositions, and arrests and releases with no further action. When less serious offenses are removed—traffic violations (except for hit and run or vehicular manslaughter), warrants with unknown charges, loitering, disturbing the peace, public nuisance, other miscellaneous misdemeanors and failure to appear—84 percent of the discharges and 82 percent of the parolees were arrested one or more times. As shown in Table 3.2, both groups experienced a mean number of 2.4 arrests during the follow-up, excluding minor offenses. The two groups therefore do not differ in percent arrested or in mean number of arrests.

Table 3-1. Number of Arrests: All Offenses

Number of Arrests	Discharges		Parolees	
	No.	%	No.	%
None	13	13.3	29	14.6
One	28	28.6	47	23.7
Two	15	15.3	36	18.2
Three	12	12.2	28	14.1
Four or more	30	30.6	58	29.3
Total	98	100.0	198	100.0
Mean	2.64		2.65	
Standard deviation	2.25		2.24	

Note: Percentages may not add to 100 due to errors in rounding.

Table 3-2. Number of Arrests: Excludes Minor Offenses

Number of Arrests	Discharges		Parolees	
	No.	%	No.	%
None	16	16.3	36	18.2
One	27	27.6	48	24.2
Two	19	19.4	33	16.7
Three	10	10.2	30	15.2
Four or more	26	26.5	51	25.8
Total	98	100.0	198	100.0
Mean	2.4		2.4	
Standard deviation	2.12		1.97	

Note: Percentages may not add to 100 due to errors in rounding.

The two groups also do not differ in time to arrests, with time measured in months. The mean number of months to the first arrest was 8.4 for the discharges and 8.1 for the parolees, which is not significant. These differences are not large, although there was a slight tendency for the discharges to be arrested somewhat sooner than the parolees for their third and fourth arrests. These data are shown in Table 3.3. The results do not differ when days instead of months are used to calculate time to arrest (data not shown).

Table 3-3. Mean Months to Separate Arrests

Arrest	Overall		Discharges			Parolees		
	Mean	S.D.	Mean	S.D.	No.	Mean	S.D.	No.
First	8.2	6.4	8.4	6.3	85	8.1	4.5	169
Second	12.2	7.0	11.5	6.8	57	12.6	7.0	122
Third	14.5	6.6	13.9	6.7	42	14.9	6.6	86
Fourth	16.4	6.2	14.9	6.5	30	17.3	6.0	58
Fifth	19.2	6.4	19.6	7.3	24	19.1	5.8	39
Sixth	17.6	5.7	17.8	5.8	8	17.6	5.8	23
Seventh	20.1	5.0	18.7	6.6	6	20.7	4.2	13
Eighth	—[a]	—	—	—	3	—	—	11
Ninth	—	—	—	—	2	—	—	4
Tenth	—	—	—	—	2	—	—	0

[a]Indicates too few cases to calculate the statistic.

But even though there is no difference between the two groups on these dimensions, it may be that the assumed effect of parole is other than on percentages arrested. Deterrence theory suggests, for example, that the celerity and severity of sanctions may affect the kind of offense committed or its seriousness. The data on this question are presented below.

Nature of Offenses

Do the two groups differ in nature of offense? For the moment we examine only overall mean scores for categories of offenses. At a later point the singular most serious charge and charge resulting in the most serious disposition will be examined.

The overall mean number of property offenses among the parolees (1.1) is slightly higher than that of the discharges (.98), although, like the remaining differences, it is insignificant (see Table 3-4). Property offenses include burglary, receiving stolen property, forgery, fraud, grand theft, petty theft, and other miscellaneous offenses. The parolees exceed the discharges in every category of property offense except petty theft.

Moreover, the parolees were slightly more likely to be charged with the more serious crimes, including homicide, rape, robbery, battery, and other assaults considered together. The overall parolee mean is .53; for the discharges it is .46. The difference is most obvious for charges of homicide and rape, of which the discharges had a total of one such charge and the parolees a total of

10. The discharges, however, lead in charges for assault with a deadly weapon and have a higher overall mean number of drug and alcohol offenses (.55) compared to the parolees (.37), which is only marginally significant. There are no differences in mean number of particular offenses per case, as shown in Table 3-5.

Table 3-4. Mean Number of Person, Property, Drug and Alcohol, to All Other Offenses

Nature of Charge	Discharges		Parolees	
	Mean	S.D.	Mean	S.D.
All person	0.46	0.83	0.53	0.88
All property	0.98	1.48	1.12	1.42
All drug and alcohol	0.55	0.98	0.37	0.81[a]
All other	0.41	0.70	0.37	0.66
N (No.)	98		198	

[a]$t = 1.55$, df = 165.6, $p < .20$

Table 3-5. Number of Offenses per Case

Nature of Charge	Discharges			Parolees		
	Mean	S.D.	No.	Mean	S.D.	No.
All person	1.45	0.85	31	1.48	0.86	71
All property	2.18	1.51	44	2.06	1.33	107
All drug and alcohol	1.59	1.05	34	1.61	0.93	46
All other	1.38	0.56	29	1.26	0.61	58

Alternative Methods

One difficulty in interpreting the results presented above is due in part to the fact that the units of observation are not independent of one another. Repeat offenders, for example, may commit a wide variety of offenses at differing time intervals and throw off calculations. In the present study, 57 percent of all arrests were charged against only 26 percent of the 296 individuals included in the study (data not shown). Thus what is needed is a summary observation for each case, not only for simplicity in understanding but also to allow for more precise statements about outcomes.

For these reasons two summary measures were taken from the follow-up data. The first is the most serious charge incurred by each individual during the entire time period of the study. If two or more charges were of equal severity (based on the severity code included in Appendix 4) the first score in time was chosen, regardless of disposition. This severity score was then matched with its corresponding charge, date of arrest, and disposition. The severity scale is discussed below.

The second summary measure was the most serious disposition received during the follow-up. Degree of seriousness was coded by using the rank order disposition code in Appendix 5,[1] making adjustments for suspended sentences and "other" dispositions on a case-by-case basis, of which there were few. If there were mixed sentences only the most serious was selected (for example, jail over probation). The most serious disposition was then matched with its corresponding charge, severity score, and date of arrest. The results using both of these methods will be discussed, beginning with the most serious charge. All minor offenses have been excluded. Both methods have been used in previous research and it is unclear what implications each has. We hope that the use of both will provide a balanced picture of outcomes.

The severity scale used in this study was developed by C.Y.A. research staff in 1978 and was adapted in part from the scale used in the Community Treatment Project (Palmer, 1974). The 9-point ranking system is based on ratings by C.Y.A. research staff and geared toward offenses frequently charged against youthful offenders. Unlike Sellin and Wolfgang's (1964) seriousness index, the present scale only requires knowledge of arrest charges. There was greater agreement on which items were higher in severity than items of lower severity. In this respect the scale does not differ from that of Rossi et al. (1974), who generally find higher variances in seriousness ratings as the crime in question decreases in seriousness.

When the most serious charge is selected, the modal offense for both groups is property-related (see Table 3-6). The parolees lead by 18 percent in these charges, particularly in burglary (22 percent) and to a lesser extent receiving stolen property and grand theft.

The second most frequent category of offense for both groups involves personal crimes, and the discharges show a slightly higher percentage in this area, particularly for battery and to a lesser extent for assault with a deadly weapon. The parolees, in contrast, were more likely to be charged with homicide and rape.

The next most frequent offense of the discharges is drug and alcohol related, and for the parolees "all other" offenses. The discharges lead the parolees by almost 9 percent in charges for under the influence, which accounts for most of the overall 10 percent difference between the two groups. The discharges also lead the parolees in all other offenses, particularly miscellaneous misdemeanor offenses and to a lesser extent otherwise uncategorizable wobblers (offenses that can be charged as either a misdemeanor or a felony).

Table 3-6. Nature of Most Serious Charge

Offense	Discharges No.	%	Parolees No.	%
Homicide	1	1.2	6	3.7
Rape	0	–	3	1.8
Assault with a deadly weapon	10	12.2	13	8.0
Robbery	6	7.3	17	10.5
Battery[a]	9	11.0	6	3.7
Other person	1	1.2	3	3.6
All person	27	32.9	48	29.6
Burglary[b]	16	19.5	51	31.5
Grand theft	4	4.9	10	6.2
Fraud	3	3.6	6	3.7
Forgery	4	4.9	7	4.3
Receiving stolen property	0	–	8	4.9
Other property	1	1.2	3	1.8
All property[c]	28	34.1	85	52.5
Marijuana	0	–	1	0.6
Dangerous drugs	4	4.9	5	3.1
Influence	10	12.2	6	3.7
All drug and alcohol[d]	14	17.1	12	7.4
Other felony	1	1.2	4	2.5
Other wobbler	3	3.6	1	0.6
Other misdemeanor	9	11.0	12	7.0
All other[e]	13	15.8	17	10.5
Total	82	100.0	162	100.0

[a] $X^2 = 4.7, p < .05$, battery versus remaining.
[b] $X^2 = 3.9, p < .05$, burglary versus remaining.
[c] $X^2 = 7.4, p < .01$, property versus remaining.
[d] $X^2 = 5.3, p < .05$, drug and alcohol versus remaining.
[e] $X^2 = 9.5, p < .01$, overall difference, collapsing drug and alcohol and other offenses.

The overall difference between the two groups when the data are categorized as person, property, and all other offenses is significant. The largest source of difference is in property offenses ($X^2 = 7.4, p < .01$) and to a lesser extent drug and alcohol related violations ($X^2 = 5.3, p < .05$). Within the category of personal offenses the discharges differ significantly in the percent charged with battery. If charges for homicide and rape are combined, the parolees are significantly more likely to have been charged with these offenses. When a correction for continuity is made the latter relationship is weaker and of borderline significance ($X^2 = 3.4, p < .10$).

For the charge resulting in the most serious disposition, property crimes are again the modal offense for both groups (32 percent discharges; 41 percent parolees). These data are shown in Table 3-7. The higher percentage of parolees charged with burglary found when selecting the most serious charge is here diminished to a 3 percent difference. The parolees lead by small percentages in all property offenses except grand theft.

Table 3-7. Nature of Charge Leading to Most Serious Disposition

Offense	Discharges		Parolees	
	No.	%	No.	%
Homicide	0	—	5	3.1
Rape[a]	0	—	3	1.8
Assault with a deadly weapon weapon	5	6.1	6	3.7
Robbery	5	6.1	19	11.7
Battery	6	7.3	5	3.1
Other person	1	1.2	3	1.8
All person	17	20.7	41	25.3
Burglary	12	14.6	29	17.9
Grand theft	0	—	4	2.5
Fraud	4	4.9	6	3.7
Forgery	7	8.5	17	10.5
Receiving stolen property	1	1.2	6	3.7
All property	26	31.7	66	40.7
Marijuana	3	3.6	1	0.6
Dangerous drugs	8	9.8	7	4.3
Influence	14	17.0	13	8.0
Other	0	—	1	0.6
All drug and alcohol[b]	25	30.5	22	13.6
Other felony	2	2.4	10	6.2
Other wobbler	3	3.6	3	1.8
Other misdemeanor	9	11.0	20	12.0
All other	14	17.1	33	20.4
Total	82	100.0	162	100.0

[a]X^2 = 4.4, p < .05; corrected X^2 = 3.5, p > .05 < .10 for homicide and rape versus other personal charges.
[b]X^2 = 10.0, p < .001, drug and alcohol versus remaining.

The next most frequent offense of the discharges, but only slightly less frequent (31 percent), is drug and alcohol offenses, while for the parolees it is personal crimes. The discharges lead overall by 14 percent in drug and alcohol offenses. There are 9 percent differences in under the influence and 3 percent to 5 percent differences in marijuana and dangerous drugs. The parolees, in contrast, lead percentage-wise in charges for homicide, rape, and robbery but have somewhat fewer offenses for battery and assault with a deadly weapon.

Finally, the two groups are fairly similar in all other offenses, the least frequent offenses of the discharges, except that the parolees were charged with a higher percentage of other felonies (4 percent) than the discharges.

The overall difference between the two groups is, as before, significant. Most of the difference is attributable to the greater percentage of drug and alcohol violations of the discharges. There are no significant differences in charges for burglary or battery. The differences in charges for homicide and rape, when combined, are significant but weakened when corrected for continuity, as earlier.

These findings differ somewhat from those found earlier for all offenses. This is because data for all offenses were presented in broad offense categories and did not reflect differences in specific charges. Moreover, repeat offenders were charged with a wide variety of offenses and the methods used to select summary outcomes only concerned one charge. Data for all offenses were thus weighted toward the mean of repeat offenders, minimizing the differences between the two groups.

Given the differences in nature of offense one might expect the two groups to differ in severity of charges. To explore this hypothesis the charges above were converted to severity scores and a test of means undertaken for all charges and the charges resulting in conviction. There were no differences across groups in the percentages convicted using either method, both overall and by offense category.

For both methods the parolee charges resulting in conviction were significantly more severe than those of the discharges (see Table 3-8). For all of the most serious charges the difference was also significant but the difference was not strong enough to produce significance for the charge resulting in the most serious disposition.

There were no further differences on other measures of outcome, regardless of method used. This includes time to all offenses, as measured in months, and time to offenses within categories of offense. Finally, there were no overall differences in time to offenses eventually resulting in conviction (data not shown).

Cumulative Percent Arrested and Convicted

Figure 3-1 shows the cumulative percentage arrested during the 26-month follow-up. The last quarter includes only two months but will be referred to as a quarter here for ease of presentation. These data show only a very small difference in quarter 5 and some small differences during quarters 2 and 6 favoring the discharges and parolees, respectively. Table 3-9 also shows that there are differences between the two groups during quarters 2, 5, and 6 in mean number

Table 3-8. Severity of Offense by Experimental Group

Offense	Discharges			Parolees		
	Mean	S.D.	No.	Mean	S.D.	No.
Most serious charge						
All offenses	5.96	1.69	82	6.25	1.55	162[a]
Offenses leading to conviction	5.82	1.66	55	6.34	1.55	108[b]
Charge leading to most serious disposition						
All offenses	5.15	1.83	82	5.51	1.79	162[c]
Offenses leading to conviction	5.08	1.87	72	5.62	1.78	145[d]

[a] $t = 2.25, p < .05$, df $= 242$
[b] $t = 1.98, p < .05$, df $= 161$
[c] $t = 1.49, p < .20$, df $= 242$
[d] $t = 2.05, p < .05$, df $= 215$

Table 3-9. Quarterly Mean Number of Arrests per Case: Less Minor Offenses

Quarter	Discharges			Parolees			t
	Mean	S.D.	No.	Mean	S.D.	No.	
1	1.48	0.77	25	1.16	0.42	51	1.96[a]
2	1.33	0.82	17	1.25	0.58	44	n.s.
3	1.32	0.61	28	1.33	0.60	45	n.s.
4	1.16	0.38	19	1.09	0.29	45	n.s.
5	1.08	0.27	26	1.48	0.77	42	3.1[b]
6	1.33	0.84	18	1.15	0.44	34	n.s.
7	1.24	0.54	21	1.27	0.58	45	n.s.
8	1.25	0.45	16	1.37	0.70	41	n.s.
9	1.06	0.25	16	1.36	0.73	28	1.94[c]

[a] $p = .06$, separate variance estimate, df $= 31.1$
[b] $p = .003$, separate variance estimate, df $= 55.4$
[c] $p = .06$, separate variance estimate, df $= 36.4$

of arrests among those who were arrested at least once. The largest difference occurs during quarter 5 ($t = 3.1, p < .003$), favoring the discharges. Overall, except for these fluctuations the data suggest that parole supervision does not reduce the number of arrests, time to arrests, or intensity of offending behavior coming to the attention of officials.

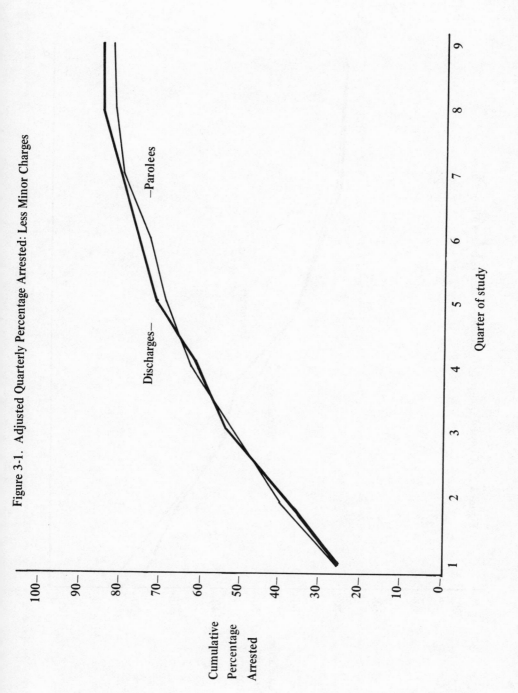

Figure 3-1. Adjusted Quarterly Percentage Arrested: Less Minor Charges

43

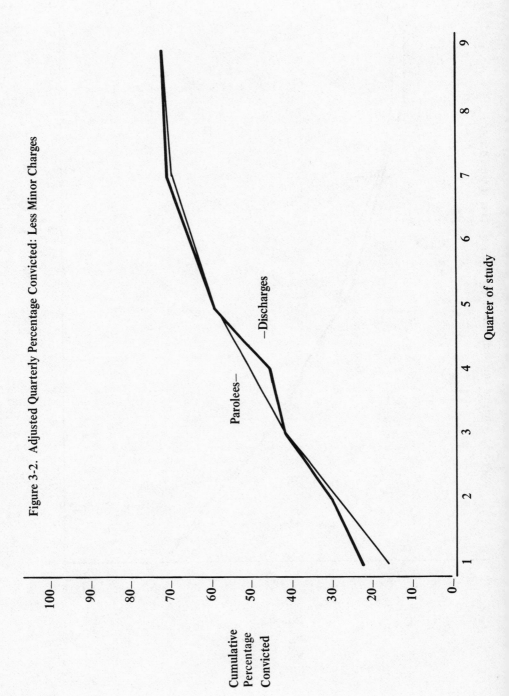

Figure 3-2. Adjusted Quarterly Percentage Convicted: Less Minor Charges

44

Another measure of recidivism is conviction. This view is particularly relevant to studies of parole because of the possibility that either the police or parole authorities arrest parolees more frequently than nonparolees (Lerner, 1977; Tittle, 1975).

The data indicate that the percentages convicted are similar just as the percentages arrested are similar. Figure 3-2 shows that fully 72 percent of the discharges and 71 percent of the parolees were convicted at least once during the follow-up period.

Correction for the Number at Risk in the Community

One problem in studying recidivism is that an offender who is arrested and incarcerated is generally not at risk to commit a further offense thereafter. If the measure of recidivism is arrest, for example, he or she will appear to be crime-free, whereas in fact the individual will simply have had no opportunity to commit additional crimes. To take account of this possible bias the data presented above were recomputed to reflect the percentage arrested who were actually at risk of being arrested. To do this the number of individuals not in custody was collected on a monthly basis. The number not in custody per month was then summed over each quarter. The number of discharges at risk during quarter 1 was 289; in other words, an average of 96.3 were not in custody per month (see Table 3-10). The number arrested was similarly summed over each quarter. The percentage arrested thus equals the number arrested per quarter divided by the number at risk as defined above.

Table 3-10. Quarterly Percentage Arrested Correcting for Number at Risk: Less Minor Offenses

Quarter	Discharges			Parolees		
	At risk	No. with arrest	% with arrest	At risk	No. with arrest	% with arrest
1	289	30	10.4	581	56	9.6
2	273	21	7.7	551	53	9.6
3	265	32	12.1	512	50	9.8
4	253	21	8.3	470	45	9.6
5	256	28	10.9	463	57	12.3
6	250	21	8.4	463	37	8.0
7	243	22	9.0	481	52	10.8
8	236	20	8.5	488	48	9.8
9	159	15	9.4	317	31	9.8

The parolees spent a higher overall mean number of months in custody (4.2) than the discharges (3.4), for reasons discussed later (data not shown here; see Chapter 5). When the table is percentaged in the manner described above, the percentage differences between the two groups are not greater by more than 3 percent during any quarter. When the data are broken down by month the percentage arrested is more variable (data not shown). However, the present data were deemed sufficient for summary purposes. These findings further substantiate the general conclusion of no great difference in the likelihood of arrest during the follow-up.

Geographical Location of Arrests

It could be argued that since the discharges were free of the parole obligations, they would leave the study area or state. The data reported here would then underestimate the extent of the discharge's crime. While this is possible, two points are worthy of note. First, more serious out-of-state charges and convictions for both groups did, in fact, appear on the rap sheets during the study period an equal percentage of the time.[2] After the study period the C.I.I. changed its policies. Second, as shown in Table 3-11, the community or county of arrests which were reported on the rap sheets are very similar between the two groups. Nonetheless, if the out-of-state arrests were of a less serious nature and if they occurred, the percentage of discharges arrested may be lower than shown here.

Table 3-11. Community of Arrest: All Arrests

Community[a]	Discharges		Parolees	
	No.	%	No.	%
Unknown	32	12.4	79	15.0
Alameda County	134	51.7	282	53.7
Martinez	30	11.6	53	10.1
Richmond	18	6.9	23	4.4
San Francisco	13	5.0	18	3.4
Oakland	2	0.8	11	2.1
All other	30	11.6	59	11.2
Total	259	100.0	525	100.0

[a]There is overlap between categories. The data were recorded as close to the place of arrest as possible. No city or county had greater than 5 percent in the "all other" category.

Note: Percentages may not add to 100.0 due to errors in rounding.

Finally, I have assumed that the discharges would be most inclined to flee the study area. Actually, some anecdotal material and official attention are focused on parolees who abscond *because* they are on parole (see, for example, the fictional account in Bunker, 1973). There is, by definition, a lack of attention paid to discharged parolees who flee their previous jurisdiction unless they are registered sex offenders or narcotics users.[3] It may be that the discharges were the least likely to leave the study area, but these comments can only be speculative.

The Discharge of Parolees

Research on the effects of parole supervision has not usually studied the discharge of parolees during follow-ups, largely because the nature or timing of discharge has been used as an indicator of the effectiveness of community supervision compared to incarceration, small caseloads versus large ones, differing supervisory styles, etc. Studies comparing prisoners held until maximum expiration of term with parolees have occasionally noted the problem (Waller, 1974), but the number of cases affected has usually been so small as not to interfere with the analysis of data.

The problem of parolee discharge from parole in the present study is especially noteworthy because the individuals were not new releases from institutions. One would therefore expect a high percentage of the parolee cases to be discharged from parole during the follow-up period since their status in relation to the parole board was not contingent upon participation in the experiment. I have not learned of any instance where inclusion in the project was used as a criterion for retaining or discharging any of the parolees from parole.

By the end of the follow-up period fully 73 percent of the 198 individuals retained on parole had been discharged (data not shown). On the face of it such attrition might appear to seriously challenge the interpretations thus far. However, inspection of the data suggests the implicit criticism is premature or at least that the issue is more complex than casual observation might suggest.

First, 69 percent of all the parolee arrests, 67 percent of the arrests excluding minor offenses, and 70 percent and 72 percent of the convictions for these respective arrests occurred while the parolees were actually on parole. Thus the bulk of official law violation of the parolees occurred while they were on parole, as shown in Table 3-12. An alternative way to state this is that 95 percent of the 53 parolees who were on parole as of the end of the follow-up had at least one arrest sometime during the follow-up (data not shown). Since many parolees had more than one arrest what is needed is some idea of the subsequent records of the parolees before and after their discharge from parole. We need to know, for example, whether the arrest or conviction which was used as a criterion for rearrest in results presented in Figures 3-1 and 3-2 was incurred before or after discharge from parole. Thus attention will be directed here to

Table 3-12. Quarterly Attrition of Individuals by Arrest or Conviction, with Percentage of Parolee Arrests Accounted for by Discharged Parolees: Less Minor Offenses

| | Actual Parolees | | | | Discharged Parolees | | | |
| | Arrests | | Convictions | | Arrests | | Convictions | |
Quarter No.	% with arrest	cum. % arrest	% with convict.	cum. % convict.	% with arrest	cum. % arrest	% with convict.	cum. % convict.
	(118)		(44)		(108)		(33)	
1	9.3	24.7	5.4	15.2	0.4	1.0	0.2	0.5
2	5.8	36.9	4.8	26.8	0.7	2.5	0.4	1.5
3	5.0	45.4	4.2	35.4	2.6	7.1	1.7	5.0
4	4.3	51.0	3.6	41.4	2.7	10.6	2.1	8.6
5	2.9	54.0	4.0	47.0	3.4	14.1	2.2	11.6
6	3.3	57.1	3.4	51.0	1.7	15.6	1.3	12.1
7	2.6	59.1	2.9	54.0	5.3	19.7	1.4	13.6
8	0.9	59.6	0.6	54.5	3.4	21.7	1.7	15.2
9	0.0	59.6	0.0	54.5	1.4	22.2	0.9	15.6

determining how many new arrests and convictions occurred for the parolees while they were on and off parole during the entire follow-up period.

Interestingly enough, the two groups are fairly similar in relative percentages arrested throughout the study period. The percentages never exceed 5 percent for all arrests; in the last quarter the parolees exceed the discharges. In five of the quarters the two groups are quite similar. When minor offenses are removed, comparisons of relative percentages arrested and convicted are not so similar as noted above, although the data on convictions are closer for the two groups than for arrests.[4]

Clearly these results do not indicate that the parolees retained on parole did "better" than those discharged. Were it possible to know which discharge cases would have been discharged from parole had they actually been retained on parole, the findings for the discharges would likely have looked very much like that found for the parolees.

Adjustments for Number at Risk in the Community

Lipton, Martinson, and Wilks (1975) point out that few studies attempt to determine whether experimental programs have their intended effects after their termination. Were the parolees discharged from parole during the follow-up arrested or convicted at a greater frequency than parolees retained on parole? An appropriate base for computing percentages is the number of randomly assigned parolees not in custody during a quarter. Where previous discussion attempted to determine the timing of arrest or conviction—whether or not it occurred on parole—the purpose here is to understand whether parolees discharged from parole differed from parolees retained on parole and the discharges in their overall number of arrests and convictions, adjusting for the number at risk.

Two trends are of interest in the findings (see Table 3-13). First, except for the first and third quarters the parolees out-percentage the discharges in arrests by between 3 percent and 6 percent per quarter (compare Table 3-7 with Table 3-4). One would expect this, since the parolees arrested were more likely to have been retained on parole, other things being equal (such as time in jurisdiction). We can no more accept this finding as showing the ineffectiveness of parole than we could the earlier one that the discharges did worse when discharged parolee arrests were excluded from comparisons.

Second, it is also evident that as the number of discharged parolees at risk grows the percentage arrested per quarter also increases. In fact, one cannot help be impressed with the basic similarity of discharged parolees and the discharges during the last six quarters of the study.

Table 3-13. Quarterly Percentage Arrested or Convicted Correcting for Number at Risk in the Community: Less Minor Offenses

Quarter	Actual Parolees				Discharged Parolees			
	Arrests		Convictions		Arrests		Convictions	
	At risk	% with arrest	At risk	% with convict.	At risk	% with arrest	At risk	% with convict.
1	539	10.2	539	8.3	42	2.4	42	2.4
2	469	10.7	469	5.1	82	3.6	82	4.9
3	369	10.8	369	6.5	143	7.0	143	5.6
4	276	12.7	276	7.6	194	5.2	194	4.1
5	222	17.6	222	10.8	241	7.5	241	5.0
6	192	11.4	192	7.8	271	5.5	271	2.2
7	164 —	14.0	164	4.3	317	9.1	317	6.3
8	145	12.4	145	10.3	343	8.7	343	4.4
9	77	18.2	77	20.8	240	7.1	240	1.7

SUMMARY

In summary, we can conclude that: 1. there are no large or systematic differences between the two groups with respect to quarterly percentages arrested or convicted per quarter, even when adjusting for the number of individuals known to be in custody; 2. there are no large or systematic differences when exclusions are made for previous arrests or convictions; 3. the parolees who were discharged from parole during the study period accounted for less than a third of all the parolee arrests and convictions but as the number of discharged parolees grew the percentages arrested and convicted approximated that of the originally assigned discharges. One would therefore expect that the differences existing between the discharged parolees and discharges will disappear over time as more parolees are discharged; and 4. the parolees were convicted of more severe offenses, regardless of method used, reflecting the greater percentage of serious personal charges brought against them and the higher percentage of drug- and alcohol-related charges brought against the discharges.

OFFENDERS AND OFFENSES

Some researchers feel that correctional treatment is more or less effective for certain categories of offenders. The question at this point is whether certain categories of parolees and discharges were more or less likely to perform differently on the various outcomes. First we examine data for all offenses (excluding minor ones) and then proceed to the most serious charge and the charge leading to the most serious disposition.

Overall Arrests and Convictions

There are several patterns of interest in overall outcomes among selected categories of offenders. The first is that even though the two groups have similar percentages arrested, the age groupings from which the offenses were generated differ. Only 27 percent of the discharges' arrests and 41 percent of the parolees' were among those 21 to 25 years of age. At the younger end of the age distribution, 28 and 17 percent of the respective group's offenses were for those 14 to 18 years of age (data not shown).

But this general observation masks important differences in the nature of offenses by age. Parolees 25 years and older were over 31 percent more likely than the discharges in this category to be charged with property offenses (see Table 3-14). Discharges in this category, in contrast, were 21 percent more likely than the parolees to be charged with drug- and alcohol-related offenses. Both differences are statistically significant. However, the greater percentage of younger discharges charged with personal offenses is not significant. In

Table 3-14. Nature of Offense by Age as of March 1, 1976

Nature of Offense	Discharges (age)			Parolees (age)		
	14-18	19-20	21-25	14-18	19-20	21-25
No.	(22)	(39)	(37)	(29)	(78)	(91)
Personal (%)	59.1	20.5	27.0	37.9	33.3	37.4
Property (%)	63.6	56.4	18.9	55.2	57.7	50.5[a]
Drug and alcohol (%)	27.3	30.8	43.2	24.1	24.4	23.1[b]
All others (%)	41.8	38.5	24.3	37.9	24.2	27.5

[a] $X^2 = 10.8, p < .01.$
[b] $X^2 = 5.2, p < .01$

Note: Percentages do not total 100% because some individuals were charged with more than one offense.

Table 3-14 there is an inverse relationship between age and personal and property offenses for the discharges but the percentage of parolees arrested for these offenses remains relatively constant across categories of age. The data thus suggest that a parole status acts to maintain tendencies to commit property offenses among older offenders and diminish the likelihood of drug- and alcohol-related offenses.

Analogous results are found when offenses are crossclassified by prior months spent on parole, shown in Table 3-15. Almost 47 percent of the discharges with 2 to 6 months prior parole were charged with a personal offense while only 20 percent were so charged among those with 19 or more months, a 27 percent difference. In contrast, the parolee percentages remained relatively constant across categories of age—in the mid-30 percent range. None of the differences across groups are significant, however. The results for property offenses are similar but not as strong.

The findings for convictions parallel those for arrests. Discharge percentages convicted for personal and property offenses decrease as age (see Table 3-16) and prior parole (see Table 3-17) increase while the parolee percentages remain relatively constant. The significant differences found earlier for property and drug and alcohol offenses among older offenders is also found for convictions. In addition, discharged youths with 7 to 18 months prior parole showed a significantly higher percentage convicted of drug and alcohol offenses. All of the discharges in this category of prior parole were convicted of the offenses with which they had been originally charged, unlike the parolees.

To control for the effects of other factors on the relationship between age and offenses, regression analyses were performed on youths 21 years and older. Both the number of property and drug and alcohol convictions were regressed on experimental assignment (which was dummy coded) and other variables (prior record, court of commitment, base expectancy score, race, and prior parole time) were added to the equation to determine whether the bivariate relationships changed.

In the equation predicting number of property convictions the b coefficient representing the effect of assignment to parole ($b = .397$; $F = 10.4$; $p < .05$) did not change when controls were added. When number of drug and alcohol convictions was regressed on assignment to discharge from parole the b for experimental assignment ($b = .197$; $F = 3.1$; $p < .10$) increased slightly to .215 ($F = 3.4$; $p < .10$) when the other variables were controlled for.

A separate regression was performed for youths with 7 to 18 months prior parole to determine whether the effect of experimental assignment changed after controlling for other variables. The b for group assignment was reduced from .141 to .125 when the effects of age, base expectancy score, race, prior record, and court of commitment were controlled for. The effect of discharge assignment in this case is therefore trivial.

Table 3-15. Nature of Offense by Prior Parole as of March 1, 1976

Nature of Offense	Discharges (prior parole)			Parolees (prior parole)		
	2-6	7-18	19 +	2-6	7-18	19 +
No.	(32)	(26)	(40)	(56)	(90)	(52)
Personal (%)	46.9	30.8	20.0	37.5	35.6	34.6
Property (%)	53.1	34.6	42.5	55.4	52.2	55.8
Drug and alcohol (%)	37.5	30.8	35.0	21.4	20.0	32.7
All others (%)	37.5	38.5	22.5	30.4	28.9	28.8

Note: Percentages do not total 100% because some individuals were charged with more than one offense.

Table 3-16. Percent Convicted by Offense and Age as of March 1, 1976

Nature of Offense	Discharges (age)			Parolees (age)		
	14-18	19-20	21-25	14-18	19-20	21-25
No.	(22)	(39)	(37)	(29)	(78)	(91)
Personal (%)	40.9	15.4	18.9	24.1	24.2	26.4
Property (%)	50.0	43.6	10.8	37.9	44.9	39.6[a]
Drug and alcohol (%)	22.7	25.6	32.4	10.3	17.9	15.4[b]
All others (%)	22.7	15.4	18.9	31.0	17.9	17.6

[a]$\chi^2 = 10.1, p < .01$
[b]$\chi^2 = 4.7, p < .05$

Note: Percentages do not total 100% because some individuals were charged with more than one offense.

Table 3-17. Percent Convicted by Offense and Prior Parole as of March 1, 1976

Nature of Offense	Discharges (prior parole)			Parolees (prior parole)		
	2-6	7-18	19 +	2-6	7-18	19 +
No.	(32)	(26)	(40)	(56)	(90)	(52)
Personal (%)	28.1	26.9	15.0	28.6	25.6	21.2
Property (%)	43.7	26.9	27.5	41.1	41.4	42.3
Drug and alcohol (%)	25.0	30.8	27.5	16.1	12.2[a]	21.2
All other (%)	28.1	15.4	12.5	23.2	20.0	15.4

[a] $X^2 = 5.7, p < .05$

Note: Percentages do not total 100% because some individuals were charged with more than one offense.

The remaining differences in overall outcomes are by risk level and to a lesser extent race. Risk level is defined by the youth's base expectancy score, a parole risk indicator that ranges from 1 (low) to 5 (high). Low risk discharges showed a lower overall mean number of convictions (including minor offenses) than the parolees but not when minor offenses were excluded (data not shown). However, discharges in this category showed a significantly lower overall mean number of serious property offenses (see Table 3-18). This finding holds when controls are made for age, prior record, prior parole, and race. The b for discharge group assignment ($b = -.431$; $F = 7.3$; $p < .05$) decreases to $-.374$ after controls are added to the equation, but it is still significant. White discharges were less likely to have any record of convictions, but this difference diminishes when less serious offenses are excluded.

Table 3-18. Overall Mean Number of Property Offenses by Base Expectancy Score 1 (Low)

Offense	Discharges			Parolees		
	Mean	S.D.	No.	Mean	S.D.	No.
Property	.42	.93	24	.98	1.1	54

$t = 2.2$; $p < .05$; $df = 76$

Comparisons were also made of whether any time was spent in custody during the follow-up. These data show that the discharges with no prior record and those with a record of delinquent contacts only were less likely than similar parolees to have spent any time in custody ($X^2 = 5.0$; $p < .05$). Low risk discharges were likewise less likely to have spent any time in custody but the difference is borderline ($X^2 = 3.7$; $p < .06$); the finding is nonetheless consistent with prior analysis. There were no significant differences in records of custody or mean custody time among those 21 years or older or by race (white), but the general direction of the differences suggests the parolees in these categories performed somewhat worse.

ADDITIONAL METHODS

Differences in nature of offense are more complex for the additional methods, due to the fact that they do not show the same results. The two consistent findings are that: 1. among those with a base expectancy score of one or who were 21 years and over, the parolees were more likely to be charged with property crimes and the discharges with drug and alcohol offenses; and 2. the discharges were more likely to be charged with drug and alcohol offenses among nonwhites, individuals committed to the C.Y.A. for personal offenses, no history of parole violations while on parole, adult felony commitments, 7-18 months prior parole, and first commitments to the C.Y.A. Beyond this, the results differ by method. In general, the findings suggest that the low risk discharges were more likely to be charged with drug- and alcohol-related offenses and the parolees, when they differ at all, with property offenses (see Tables 3-19 and 3-20).

Both methods also show fairly consistent results for differences in severity of charges: parolees with low base expectancy scores performed worse than the discharges, as did those with a prior record of contacts only, although the latter relationship is weak for the charge leading to the most serious disposition. Similarly, although the most serious charge severity is significantly different for those 21 years and older, with the parolees performing worse, the difference for the charge resulting in the most serious disposition is on the borderline of significance. The remaining differences in types of offenses and severity scores are not consistent across method.

CHAPTER SUMMARY

There are no large and systematic differences between the two groups in arrest and conviction record, number of arrests and convictions, time to arrests overall and to those resulting in conviction, cumulative percentages arrested and convicted while correcting for the number at risk in the community, or overall time spent in custody. Evidence for differences in outcome is found instead in nature of offenses and the higher severity of parolee charges. Moreover, certain categories of offenders were found to perform more or less positively depending upon what outcome measure is examined. Older parolees were more likely to be charged and convicted of property offenses while older discharges were more likely to be convicted of drug and alcohol offenses. Low risk discharges were also less likely to be convicted of property crimes than the parolees.

Table 3-19. Summary Table of Differences in Nature of Offense
and Severity Scores by Background Characteristics
for the Two Methods

| Background Characteristics | Most Serious Charge | | |
| | Discharges worse in: | Parolees worse in: | |
	Drug/alcohol	Property	Severity
All nonwhites	X	X	X
13-24 months remaining in jurisdiction		X	
Personal offender	X		
No parole violations	X	X	
Never married	X	X	X
Adult felony commitments	X	X	X
Base expectancy 1	X	X	X
Age 21 and over	X[a]	X	X
7-18 months prior parole	X		X
First commitment	X		
13 or more months in institutions	X[b]		
25-36 months remaining in jurisdiction	X[c]	X	
6-8 months in institutions		X	
Prior record of commitment only		X	
Richmond parole unit	X[b]		

[a]Also differed in all other offenses.
[b]Differed in drug and alcohol and others combined but not separately.
[c]Also differed in personal offenses.

Table 3-20. Summary Table of Differences in Nature of Offense and Severity Scores by Background Characteristics for the Two Methods

| Background Characteristics | Charge Leading to the Most Serious Disposition | | |
| | Discharges worse in: | Parolees worse in: | |
	Drug/alcohol	Property	Severity
All nonwhites	X		
13-24 months remaining in jurisdiction	X		X
Personal offender	X		
No parole violations	X		
Never married	X		
Adult felony commitments	X		
Base expectancy 1	X	X	
Age 21 and over	X	X	
7-18 months prior parole	X		
First commitment	X		X
13 or more months in institutions	X	X[a]	
Richmond parole unit	X		
Whites	X		
9-12 months in institutions	X		
Non-personal or property offender	X		
Juvenile commitment	X		
37 or more months remain in jurisdiction			X

[a]Parolees differ significantly in personal crimes.

NOTES

1. See Appendix 5, Disposition Code.
2. Data not shown. It is included in the "all other" category of Table 3-5.
3. See the conclusion section entitled, "The Illusion of Control," where this issue is discussed in more general terms.
4. Data shown in Table 3-6 are for charges less minor offenses.

4
The Limits of
Social Control

When agencies of social control collect and generate statistics on individuals and groups and perform tasks which may directly or indirectly affect their welfare, their activities are constrained not only by time, money, and existing exchange relationships, as well as by sources of legitimation and/or constitutionally guaranteed liberties of individuals. But when civil authority is vested in a parole agency, with independent powers allowing it to define the nature and extent of civil liberties of its charges without judicial review, and is granted means of enforcing them through arrest or additional restrictions on liberty, it becomes less clear what the limits of social control are or can be. It was this underlying distrust of an independent civil authority which prompted European criticism of the indeterminate sentence and parole in the United States (United States Department of Justice, 1939). The parole function has only recently been subjected to significant review by the courts, resulting in a recognition of prisoner's rights and changes in revocation practices (Orland, 1975).

The purpose of this chapter is to assess the limits to parole practices that generate spurious recidivism. In some ways this takes us to the heart of the methodological aspect of the paradox of social control represented by parole: due to the individual's placement under the jurisdiction of an agency with independent civil authority, the parolee can be arrested and reimprisoned by parole agents without the same restrictions applicable to free citizens; this is the main structural source of spurious recidivism discussed in Chapter 1. The fact that this can and does occur is one roadblock to understanding the consequences of social control.

Previous research (Lerner, 1977) has not seriously considered the question of how arrest outcome measures are affected by the actions of parole officers, above and beyond that of other criminal justice processing agencies.

While some previous work in this area has used outcome information taken from parole authority files (for example, parole violations, revocations, nature of discharge from parole), this study does not use these outcome data due in part to the fact that the discharges have no such information collected on them but also because past research has found them to be biased (Lerman, 1972).

Nonetheless, as shown in Chapter 5, a small number of parolees were returned to institutions in this study through revocation of parole for a technical violation of parole. This reflects the policy and, from all indications, the actual practice in the C.Y.A., which is to allow the court to complete its fact-finding and adjudicative function and then for the parole board to take any action it deems necessary. The long-standing practice in the C.Y.A. of informally agreeing with prosecutors on revocation actions can still be found but it appears to be much less prominent than in the past.

During the time period of the present study, for example, there were 29 parole returns for purely technical violations of the rules of parole for Zone I in the state (excluding out-of-state cases) in which the study group cases were located. This amounts to an average of approximately 3.2 revocations for every three months or 1.1 per month. The average daily population on parole during this period was 1,750 in Zone I, and the overall rate of violation per 100 parolees for technicals was .0006 during the study period.

The "hands off" policy of the C.Y.A. is also reflected in the lack of parole agent participation in the plea bargaining process. This state of affairs differs greatly from that described by McCleary's (1978) recent study of (adult) parole agent participation in plea bargaining in Illinois. During the course of the present study, I uncovered not one instance of direct participation by agents in this process. As pointed out in Chapter 2, however, the use of parole holds, making bail impossible, may well indirectly structure the available strategies and resources of the parolee. So, too, might the recommendations made by agents to probation officers on parolee progress on parole.

AGENT PARTICIPATION
IN THE ARREST-DISPOSITION PROCESS

The depiction of parole agent or board participation in the justice process as largely a *post hoc* adjudicative activity presented above is even more relevant to the arresting behavior of parole agents. If Lerner's (1977) assumption that agents play a significant role in the arrest process were true, one would expect them to arrest parolees more often than is shown in previous research. Past research has been almost exclusively concerned with adults and neither youthful offenders nor with C.Y.A. practices, and leads one to assume that the proclivity of agents to arrest parolees is quite variable in time and place.

The work of Minor and Courlander (1979) identifies a specific point in time at which parole itself may spuriously generate "crime." They argue that parolee violations show an increase during the first weeks and months on parole because: 1. violations increase as the frequency of contact with agents increases[1] ; and 2. the number of contacts with agents is greatest during the first months on parole. However, my argument is that the findings of existing research do not offer strong or consistent support for this speculation or Lerner's.

Using the logic of Minor and Courlander (1979) it is difficult to explain away the findings of the present study on grounds of official bias. If official biases are more likely to be introduced during the first months on parole, then it is not clear why the discharges had slightly more arrests among those with two to six months prior parole. Moreover, it is difficult to explain why the parolees with longer months of prior parole time had somewhat higher percentages of arrests than the discharges. This brings one to the question of what the arrest statistics mean: are they a function of deterrence, labeling, organizational processing, or something else?

To clarify these issues, I review the findings of three studies of the sources of violation reports—documents filed by agents which *could* result in revocation of parole, a study of the time distribution of parole agents in the C.Y.A., and materials gathered from interviews with parole agents in the study area.

Information Sources for Violation Reports

Takagi (1967), Studt (1973), and Star, Berecochea, and Petrocchi (1978) collected information on the information source from which officers make recommendations to the parole board for disposition of parole violations. All of the studies were conducted in California. Table 4-1 shows the source of information for these violation reports by each study.

The source of information has been classified as internal or external to the parole agency since the issue is the extent to which agents independently discover "crime." Most of the information came from sources other than the parole agent, and predominantly from the police. If one were to exclude drug cases—and in the present study there are very few such cases—the role of parole agents in the arrest process is minimal. Unfortunately Star, Berecochea, and Petrocchi (1978) were not able to distinguish agent-instigated arrests for drugs —a *visible* law violation, unlike most—from other criminal charges. In any case, most information on the law violational behavior of parolees is uncovered external to the parole agency.[2] Moreover, it is an open question whether drug violations would have been discovered by the police anyway.

These data offer little support for the agent-intervention hypothesis or assumption for nondrug offenses. The information is dated, except perhaps for that of Star, Berecochea, and Petrocchi (1978), a study which actually spanned an eight-year period, does not control for actual parolee behavior, and may not reflect current practices or changes brought about by the *Morrissey* decision.

Table 4-1. Information Source for Violation Reports (in Percent)

Information Source	Study		
	Takagi	Studt	Star et al.[a]
No.	(1,023)	(90)	(8,883)
External Source	94.7	83.0	87.0
Police	71.2	65.0	87.0[b]
Narcotics testing	14.1	13.0	—[e]
Family	9.4	5.0	—[e]
Internal Source	5.3	17.0	13.0
Parolee	2.4	1.5	—[e]
Parole agent	2.9	15.5[c]	13.0[d]
Total	100.0	100.0	100.0

[a]Includes only those cases involving an arrest (excludes 608 cases).

[b]1,876 cases or 21.1% of the total were the result of citizen calls to the police. Viewing the police as responsible for the arrest raises the percentage of police initiated arrests from 65.9 to 87%.

[c]Includes ten absconders, three cases of agent discovery of drug usage, and one case of no monthly report.

[d]Includes only agent-issued arrests; the nature of the charge was not identified in this study.

[e]Data not collected separately.

Additional evidence bearing directly on the question of whether increased surveillance (contacts) during the early months on parole results in an increase in returns to prison is also found in Star, Berecochea, and Petrocchi (1978). If agent/board actions are measured by the percentage of parolees returned to prison while controlling for prior time spent on parole, we find that the percent returned to prison decreases only slightly as time on parole increases, apparently offering some indirect support for Minor and Courlander. But the relationship is very weak, as shown in Table 4-2.

An alternative way to examine the thesis is to look at the number of violation reports per 100 parolees per quarter by their length of time spent on parole. These data are shown in Table 4-3.[3] The trend is obvious: those with the shortest amount of time on parole, less than one year, and hence with more contacts or surveillance have lower violation rates than those with between one and less than three years of parole. Those with three or more years are slightly lower than those with one year or less. The evidence presented here does not offer consistent or strong support for the argument that spurious recidivism is generated during early months on parole at the level of arrest. Nor is it clear that the hypothesis can be tested without an independent measure of crime.

Table 4-2. Percentage of Total Parole Board Actions by Nonsuspended Time on Parole

Nonsuspended Time on Parole	No.	Percentage of Total Board Actions		
		Return to Prison	Continue on Parole	Other
6 months or less	2,014	44.5	50.5	5.0
6 months to 1 year	2,658	43.8	51.2	5.0
1 year to 2 years	3,037	41.2	53.2	5.6
2 years to 3 years	1,242	37.6	54.4	8.0
3 or more years	586	36.7	56.5	6.8
Total	9,537[a]	41.8	52.5	5.7

[a]Excluded are 26 cases for whom this information was not recorded (9,563 − 26 = 9,537).

Source: Star, Berecochea, and Petrocchi, *Return to Prison Ordered: Policy in Practice and Change.* Sacramento: California Department of Corrections (unpublished manuscript, 1978).

Table 4-3. Violation Reports per Quarter by Length of Time on Present Parole

Time on Present Parole	Violation Rate[a]
Less than 1 year	7.6
1 year but less than 2	8.1
2 years but less than 3	10.0
3 years or longer	6.6
Overall	7.9

[a]The number of violation reports per quarter per 100 parolees.

Source: Star, Berecochea, and Petrocchi, *Return to Prison Ordered: Policy in Practice and Change.* Sacramento: California Department of Corrections (unpublished manuscript, 1978).

So Much Crime, So Little Time

Another, less mentioned, fact related to surveillance activities of parole officers is that agents have little time to independently uncover law violations on the part of parolees. As Davis (1975, p. 8) has shown in her rigorous study of the time distribution of parole officers in the C.Y.A., the amount of time spent in violation investigations has increased substantially since around 1972 due to bureaucratization of parole work. These changes have resulted in less

time for "direct services" to wards, including supervision, and presumably surveillance, of parolees. Since caseload supervision constitutes the only category
of "direct services . . . which represents a discretionary usage of time," it is not
surprising that this function accounted for the decrease of all "direct service"
activities. Some full-time violations officers, individuals located in most parole
units who only conduct violations investigations, are quick to point out that
35 to 45 percent of staff time and money resources are expended on violation
procedures that involve only 10 percent of those on parole. Thus, what time
could be used for surveillance purposes has decreased and there has been an
increase in time spent on violations investigations.

The general pattern we see in these data is that the activities C.Y.A. agents
engage in that relate to criminal behavior are reactive rather than proactive to
charges brought against parolees by others. *Parole officer time is shaped by the
structural contingencies of the violation process itself after a parolee has been
arrested by the police.* It is indeed at the level of disposition that parole agents
or a parolee status may play an important role in a parolee's career. Irwin's
(1970) discussion of "banking" and McCleary's (1978) depiction of agent discretion as affected by the structural constraints imposed by *Morrissey* are
consistent with this interpretation of agent work.

Parole Agent Interpretations

To what extent do parole officers report arresting or assisting in the arrest
of parolees? To gain a more complete understanding of the situation, I interviewed all available parole officers who worked in the study area during the
time period of the follow-up. The answer to the general question of whether
parole agents played a significant role in the arrest of parolees was unanimous:
parole agents rarely instigate arrests or cooperate with police in an arrest. Most
noted that agents had instigated arrests at one point or another or had coopera-
ted with the police in making an arrest, but those incidents were well-remem-
bered and very infrequent. Admittedly these views may be self-serving but their
consideration appears warranted here.

Responses to queries as to why such instances did not occur more often
were again almost unanimous: parole officers in the study area considered
themselves to be ward advocates and thought the police were in many cases
insensitive to ward needs and problems. One unit supervisor stated:

> We don't carry guns; we are trying to help them. Many parole offi-
> cers are hostile toward the police, at least in this area. On occasion
> we take the ward's statement over the police's in making violation
> reports; when making violation reports we rarely or never talk to
> the arresting officer. We used to reward parole agents who showed
> "sympathy and understanding of wards" on our routine evaluation

of agents, but never did we get evaluated on "sympathy and understanding of the police."

An agent who had once been a police officer responded that parole agents are not adequately trained in how to arrest someone and feel uncomfortable in doing so. Others expressed the feeling that assisting the police or arresting a parolee alone would not only be potentially dangerous but also might create more danger because the parole officer has developed a relationship with the parolee which is purportedly noncoercive and open. Most admitted that some agents liked to play "cop" but that they were concentrated in rural areas.

While there is of course room to doubt this somewhat nostalgic picture of a warm-hearted social worker befriending his or her charge,[4] the point is that there appears to be little or no organizational reinforcement or incentive for agents to play "cop." In some rural areas, where agents view the police as a reference group or significant other, this may well not be true.

Seeming proactive actions, such as the issuance of a warrant, emanate from board directives and are in most cases a *post hoc* action. Warrants are issued for two principle reasons: 1. so-called AWOL (absent without leave) or absconding from parole cases; and 2. detainers, which are holds upon arrest. Absconders require warrants while detainers are usually instigated when a parolee has been arrested on a "serious" charge and is already in custody. Warrants for absconders, according to agents, do not usually eventuate in arrest or serve as an instigator of arrest. Such warrants are often resolved when the parolee is arrested for a different offense, in which case the warrant serves as a "hold," or the parolee simply comes into his or her parole office and explains the absence and the warrant is removed. One somewhat cynical agent had this to say about absconders:

> Absconding cases are the best ones we have. We put out a warrant
> on them, don't see them again, and they're on active parole. And
> there aren't any violation actions to worry about unless they blow
> it. Some of these guys seem to be quite careful with themselves.
> We later discharge them at expiration with a general. If they walk
> in and explain—almost any explanation will do—the warrant is re-
> voked and everything is fine.

In other cases the agent is unable to locate an absconder but learns through others, such as family, how the individual is doing and later discharges him or her at expiration with a General, in line with policy.

In older discussions of the relationship between parolee crimes or status violations and return to prison a parole officer sometimes states, "If I applied the rules [of parole], I imagine half my caseload would be in jail" (Takagi, 1967, p. 103). But changes due to legal decisions and structural changes in correctional administration have made return of parolees for technical violations most costly. It does occur, but much less often than a decade ago.

CHAPTER SUMMARY

This chapter examines the nature of spurious recidivism, focusing on the arrest process of parolees. At issue is the extent to which parole officers inflate parolee charges above what they would be if the individual were not on parole. Previous research (Lerner, 1977; Minor and Courlander, 1979) implies or assumes that parole agents play a significant role in the arrest process.

While this may be true in some jurisdictions my point here is that, in the East Bay area of concern to this research, parole agents largely react to parolee crime detected by police and others, with the possible exception of drug offenses. Just as Studt (1973) noted some time ago, parole agents spent a good deal of time on the surveillance of parolees but discovered little crime. In future research it will be important to determine to what extent parole agents actually play a role in the arrest of parolees, rather than falling back on possible unwarranted assumptions.

In support of the argument the sources of information used for violation reports were examined for adult parolees. This information provided an indirect test of Minor and Courlander's (1979) hypotheses and questioned whether a parole officer's "invisible hand" generates spurious recidivism to the extent implied by Lerner (1977). It was also shown that parole agents in the study area have neither the time nor, apparently, the inclination or training to arrest parolees to any great extent.

NOTES

1. There is a good deal of evidence that this assumption does not hold water. See the review of the literature noted in Chapter 1, Note 4. The authors' conclusion appears to receive strongest support in studies testing the effectiveness of probation and parole programs of narcotics users, studies they cite in support of their assumption. Studies such as these are usually uninterpretable from a theoretical standpoint, however. Note Martinson, Kassebaum, and Ward's (1970, p. 648) review of one such study:

> This program assessed the effects of the use of Nalline. . . . It is not clear how the study could have avoided supporting the use of Nalline. If the recidivism rate were *lower* for the treatment group than the control group, one would say that the fear of detection by Nalline deterred men from using drugs, or at least markedly reduced drug use. On the other hand, if the treatment group had *higher* recidivism rates, the figures can be said to show that Nalline is an effective detection device resulting in the reconfinement of a larger number of drug addicts. The second alternative was indeed the finding. In either case, the program could have been found to be worth using. (Emphasis in original.)

This criticism is analogous to that levelled at parole reserarch in Chapter 1, pp. 10-11.

2. Irwin's (1970, p. 147) point, though, is well taken. He notes that the police "use the parole agency as a source of information about possible law violators." To what extent

this form of cooperation leads to arrests is an open question. Some parole agents in the study area noted that they did on occasion give information to police about such things as the address of a parolee's girlfriend or boyfriend, friends of parolees, etc. They also said that the police come to them as a last resort and that agents refuse to release information in some cases. Of course this means that the police gain information about potential non-parolee crime also, and does not speak to the issue of whether the police would eventually arrest an individual without the agency's help. This topic deserves further study.

3. Not only are the data categorized differently, but they also refer to the period before there was a conservative policy change in the California Department of Corrections. The general patterns noted below before and after the change are quite similar, however.

4. Indeed, two of the eight agents spoken to said that they "turned their backs" on parolees who got into serious or even not so serious trouble with the law. It was noted that most of the wards "do not want our help" and "want to be off parole." Whether or not agents turned their backs appeared to be related partly to the degree that agents thought the parolee had the correct "attitude." McCleary (1978) spoke in a similar context about parolee "sincerity."

5
After Conviction: Effects of Parole on Sanctioning

This chapter investigates the disparate sentencing patterns of the two groups. The results show that the parolees received more serious sentences—a pattern which does not appear to be entirely due to their more serious charges. The first section discusses the distribution of custody time in jail, C.Y.A., and adult prison during the entire follow-up period. Next, the sentencing differentials are examined and the background characteristics of those receiving various sentences shown. Finally, a multivariate approach is used to describe the greater likelihood for parolees to be sentenced to adult prison for more serious charges.

TIME IN CUSTODY

A veteran of research on parole indicates that time spent in confinement is perhaps "the most sensitive criterion" existing to assess correctional efforts to change people: "The average percentage of . . . time spent in confinement by a group of released offenders reflects the frequency, duration, and interval between their subsequent incarcerations" (Glaser, 1973, p. 23). In the present case, time spent in custody refers to jail, C.Y.A., and adult prison lockups. These data should shed some light on the nature of those in charge of custody. Not only how *much* confinement, but *who* is in charge, is an important question. As we shall see below, custody data reflect differences in sentencing upon conviction.[1]

Methods and Assumptions

Sixteen or more days in custody during a month was counted as one month. The reason for adopting the 16-day figure rather than an entire month was to have more precise data for undertaking cost benefit analysis and because it facilitated coding and calculating the number at risk in the community per quarter. If the confinement data had been coded in days the latter task would have been overly cumbersome. This method might introduce a small amount of bias into the analysis but it is not deemed to be serious. Only actually imposed sentences have been considered. The place of custody was coded for the agency in which the individual was located; if the individual was given a 12-month jail sentence but his parole was revoked and 9 months was spent in the C.Y.A., 3 months was counted as jail time and 9 months as C.Y.A. time. Only time spent in custody during the 26-month follow-up was counted.

The measure of time in confinement may be seen as a conservative but roughly accurate estimate of jail time for the parolees. However, the overall time in custody for both groups is undoubtedly higher than reported here, due in large part to unreported pretrial detention.

Findings

As noted in Chapter 3, the discharges spent a lower overall mean number of months in custody during the follow-up (3.4 months) than the parolees (4.2 months), but this difference was not statistically significant. The two groups also differed in the mean number of months in custody among those ever placed in custody as shown in Table 5-1. The discharges spent 6.9 months per case in custody and the parolees 8.2 months, statistically a weak difference ($t = 1.4, p < .20$).

Although there are no overall differences, it is interesting to examine where time was spent. Since the parolees were still under the jurisdiction of the C.Y.A. one might expect them to have spent more time there during the follow-up than the discharges. But in fact the discharges actually spent more time in the C.Y.A., while the parolees spent more time in adult prison. Both groups spent approximately equal time in jail. The overall difference between the two groups with respect to C.Y.A. and adult prison time is of borderline significance ($X^2 = 3.5, p < .10$), but the simple r between experimental status and months spent in C.Y.A. confinement is .27 ($p = .05$). Thus 7 percent of the variation in C.Y.A. time can be explained by experimental assignment alone, although the number of cases is somewhat small.

The difference in time spent in the C.Y.A. and adult prison is a result of the fact that the discharges were returned to the C.Y.A. as new commitments and such returns had longer lengths of stay than recommitments; in addition, the number of potential parolee new commitments and recommitments was

Table 5-1. Months in Custody per Case by Holding Agency

Holding agency	Discharges					Parolees[a]					Overall	
	N	No.	%	Mean	S.D.	N	No.	%	Mean	S.D.	Mean	S.D.
Jail	35	150	45.4	4.3	3.7	75	373	45.4	5.0	4.3	4.8	4.1
C.Y.A.	9	99	30.0	11.0	4.4	28	210	25.5	7.5	5.8	8.4	5.6
Adult prison	9	81	24.5	9.0	3.5	22	239	29.1	10.9	8.0	10.3	7.0
Total	53	330	100.0	6.9	5.2	125	822	100.0	8.2	6.1	7.8	5.8

[a]t-tests not significant.
Note: Percentages may not add to 100.0 due to errors in rounding.

deflated because the parolees were sentenced to adult prison more often than were the discharges. The purpose now is to understand how this state of affairs came about.

AFTER CONVICTION

Can the differential amount of time spent in the C.Y.A. compared to prison or jail be explained by the different offenses of the two groups, the severity of offenses, or some other factor or set of factors (such as age or criminal history)? To explore these questions we examine the nature of sentences for the most serious charge and the charge leading to the most serious disposition. We then ask whether sentences coincide with what would be expected given differences between the two groups in the nature and severity of offenses by selected background characteristics shown in Chapter 3. This analysis should clarify the role of parole at the level of arrest and disposition.

Disposition of the Most Serious Charge

Fully 67 percent of the charges of both groups resulted in conviction. The bulk of attrition occurred at court in the form of dismissals for both groups. The parolees did show a slightly higher percentage of charges which were dismissed at intake (data not shown).

What is of interest is the nature of dispositions after conviction, particularly for personal crimes (see Table 5-2). While the overall percentage receiving sentences of 180 days or more of jail, C.Y.A., and adult prison is fairly close (44 percent discharges compared to 52 percent parolees), the two groups differ dramatically in the distribution of these three sentences. Where the discharges were most likely to receive jail sentences of 180 days or more, followed by C.Y.A. and probation sentences, the parolees were most likely to receive adult prison sentences, followed by jail sentences of 180 days or more, shorter jail sentences, and *then* C.Y.A. sentences. The parolee-discharge difference in percentage sentenced to adult prison for personal crimes compared to all other convictions is significant.

The primary sources of difference in sentences to adult prison for the personal offenses are that 6 of the 9 homicide and rape charges of the parolees resulted in convictions to adult prison, only one in a C.Y.A. commitment, and the remainder to jail of 180 days or more (data not shown). The discharges were not convicted for any of these charges; the single charge for homicide was dropped. However, even if the homicide and rape charges are excluded from computations, significant differentials in sentencing patterns still remain. For example, 25 percent of all (28) parolee convictions for assault with a deadly weapon, robbery, and battery resulted in adult prison sentences, while none of the 17 convictions of the discharges for these offenses resulted in such a

Table 5-2. Disposition by Most Serious Charge

Disposition	Discharges						Parolees					
	Person		Property		Drugs and other		Person		Property		Drugs and other	
	No.	%	No.	%	No.	%	No.	%	No.	%	No.	%
No conviction[a]	9	33.3	10	35.7	8	29.6	10	20.8	34	40.0	10	34.5
Miscellaneous conviction, other, fine only[b]	1	3.7	0	0.0	4	14.8	0	0.0	3	3.5	7	24.1
Probation	3	11.1	3	10.7	6	22.2	3	6.2	7	8.2	3	10.3
Jail 1-29 days	0	0.0	0	0.0	5	18.5	5	10.4	5	5.9	0	0.0
Jail 30-179 days	2	7.4	3	10.7	3	11.1	5	10.4	7	8.2	3	10.3
Jail 180+ days	8	29.6	6	21.4	0	0.0	8	16.7	19	22.4	2	6.9
C.Y.A.	4	14.8	3	10.7	1	3.7	4	8.3	4	4.7	3	10.3
Adult prison[c]	0	0.0	3	10.7	0	0.0	13	27.1	6	7.0	1	3.4
Total	27	100.0	28	100.0	27	100.0	48	100.0	85	100.0	29	100.0
Percentage convicted	66.7		64.3		70.4		79.2		60.0		65.5	

[a] Includes outstanding warrants, arrest, and release and dismissed at intake and at court.
[b] Includes suspended sentences, miscellaneous sentences (for example, restitution, work in the community), and death.
[c] Includes the California Department of Corrections, California Rehabilitation Center, out-of-state and federal prison commitments.
Note: Percentages may not add to 100.0 due to errors in rounding.

sentence (data not shown). Thus, parolee personal offenses appear to have been given more punitive sentences compared to the discharges.

All of the homicide and rape charges were brought against nonwhites in the study, particularly blacks committed to the C.Y.A. for property offenses. Black parolees were, overall, somewhat more likely to be sentenced to the C.Y.A. than black discharges (see Table 5-3). There were no large differences in charges against nonwhites and whites for the remaining personal offenses.

Discharge property offenses follow a similar pattern of receiving a higher percentage of C.Y.A. sentences, but show a slightly higher percentage of adult prison sentences than the parolees (see Table 5-2). Moreover, the percentage of each group receiving stiff jail sentences is approximately the same for the two groups. However, none of the aforementioned differences found for personal offenses are significantly different here.

Drug- and alcohol-related and other offenses do show some differences in sentence patterns. The percentage convicted is quite similar (70 percent discharges compared to 66 percent for the parolees) but the parolees received a significantly greater percentage of jail sentences of 180 days or more (C.Y.A. and adult prison sentences) when these dispositions are combined and compared to all other convictions (X^2 = 4.7, p < .05, with no correction for cell sizes). Moreover, the discharges were more likely to receive probation sentences for this category of offense, a difference which is largely the result of sentences for under the influence: five of the nine convictions for discharge drug- and alcohol-related offenses received probation only; two of seven parolee offenses received probation (data not shown).

Overall, the parolees were significantly more likely to be sentenced to adult prison, a finding which holds regardless of whether the statistical test, here chi-square, is applied to charges resulting in conviction (X^2 = 5.1, p < .05) or to all charges regardless of disposition (X^2 = 4.8, p < .05).

Disposition by Severity of Charge

Crossclassification of dispositions by severity scores of each case yields a pattern of discharges receiving more lenient treatment than the parolees. When severity scores are trichotomized into low, moderate, and high, a parolee with a severity score of 7 to 9 (higher), as shown in Table 5-4, is more than three times as likely as a discharge in this category to receive an adult prison sentence. Although the percentage of parolees convicted for high severity scores was somewhat higher than that of the discharges (69 percent and 59 percent, respectively), the likelihood that a parolee in this category would be sentenced to adult prison is significant (X^2 = 4.3, p < .05). For the moderate severity scores (including scores of 4, 5, and 6), the discharges were somewhat more likely to receive lengthy jail sentences than the parolees.

When the severity scores are dichotomized, as in Table 5-5, the percentage difference in sentences to probation for charges of severity 3 to 6 (low) is re-

Table 5-3. Disposition of Most Serious Offense by Selected Background Characteristics

Disposition	Blacks only				Age 21 and over			
	Discharges		Parolees		Discharges		Parolees	
	No.	%	No.	%	No.	%	No.	%
No conviction[a]	17	36.2	36	40.0	8	29.6	23	32.4
Miscellaneous conviction, other, fine only[b]	2	4.3	1	1.0	5	18.5	5	7.0
Probation[c]	9	19.1	6	6.7	5	18.5	6	8.5
Jail 1-29 days	1	2.1	6	6.7	3	11.1	5	7.0
Jail 30-179 days	3	6.4	6	6.7	0	—	5	7.0
Jail 180+ days	9	19.1	17	18.9	4	14.8	13	18.3
C.Y.A.	1	2.1	13	14.4	0	—	1	1.4
Adult prison[d]	5	10.6	5	5.6	2	7.4	13	18.3
Total	47	100.0	90	100.0	27	100.0	71	100.0

Note: Percentages may not add to 100.0 due to errors in rounding.
[a]Includes outstanding warrants, arrest, and release and dismissed at intake and at court.
[b]Includes suspended sentences, miscellaneous sentences (for example, restitution, work in the community), and death.
[c]$\chi^2 = 4.9$, $p < .05$, probation versus all other.
[d]$\chi^2 = 5.1$, $p < .05$, adult prison versus all other. Adult prison includes the California Department of Corrections, California Rehabilitation Center, out-of-state and federal prison commitments.

Table 5-4. Disposition by Severity of Offense: Most Serious Charge

	Severity of Offense							
	Discharges				Parolees			
	4-6		7-9		4-6		7-9	
Disposition	No.	%	No.	%	No.	%	No.	%
No conviction[a]	7	24.1	16	41.0	17	36.2	31	31.3
Miscellaneous conviction, other, fine only[b]	3	10.3	0	—	5	10.6	1	1.0
Probation	4	13.8	2	5.1	8	17.0	2	2.0
Jail 1-29 days	3	10.3	0	—	4	8.5	6	6.1
Jail 30-179 days	3	10.3	5	12.8	5	10.6	9	9.1
Jail 180+ days	5	17.2	9	23.1	4	8.5	24	24.2
C.Y.A.	3	10.3	5	12.8	3	6.4	7	7.1
Adult prison[c]	1	3.4	2	5.1	1	2.1	19	19.2
Total	29	100.0	39	100.0	47	100.0	99	100.0
Percentage convicted	75.9		59.0		63.8		68.7	

[a]Includes outstanding warrants, arrest, and release and dismissed at intake and at court.

[b]Includes suspended sentences, miscellaneous sentences (for example, restitution, work in the community), and death.

[c]Includes the California Department of Corrections, California Rehabilitation Center, out-of-state and federal prison commitments.

Note: Percentages may not add to 100.0 due to errors in rounding.

versed due to inclusion of drug- and alcohol-related offenses. The discharges were somewhat more likely to receive light jail sentences and somewhat less likely to receive jail sentences in excess of 179 days.

Disposition of Charge Leading to Most Serious Disposition

The tendency for personal crimes to be treated more punitively is somewhat difficult to interpret using this method due to the small number of personal crimes of discharges. About 44 percent of the parolees received adult prison sentences for this category of offense, while only 3 of 17 or about 18 percent of the discharges did (see Table 5-6). Moreover, 24 percent of the discharges and only 10 percent of the parolees received C.Y.A. sentences. If no statistical correction for small expected values is made the difference is significant, as found earlier; when a correction is made the difference is not significant.

The source of difference in sentences to adult prison for personal crimes is found in ten convictions for robbery, four for homicide, two for rape, and two for assault with a deadly weapon among the parolees (data not shown). Only four of the parolee convictions for these offenses resulted in C.Y.A. sentences. In contrast, the discharges received two sentences to adult prison for assault with a deadly weapon and one for robbery, and the C.Y.A. commitments were accounted for by three robbery convictions and one for battery. When charges for assault with a deadly weapon, robbery, and battery are combined, the parolees were over two times more likely to receive adult prison sentences for these offenses, and the discharges two and one-half times more likely to receive C.Y.A. sentences (data not shown). The discharges were also over one and one-half times more likely to receive jail sentences of 180 days or more. The number of cases is small here, so the findings should be viewed with caution.

There are no great differences between the discharges and parolees in sentences for property offenses. Between 15 percent and 17 percent of both groups received C.Y.A. or adult prison sentences for property crimes, and the discharges were only slightly more likely to receive stiff jail sentences (again see Table 5-6). The parolees lead slightly in sentences to probation.

Drug and alcohol and all other offenses show strong differences by experimental group in sentences to probation, for reasons noted above. These data again suggest the reluctance of the court to impose a probation sentence for parolees charged with drug and alcohol offenses.

As found earlier, the overall difference between the groups in C.Y.A. sentences is not significant but the existing differences can be attributed to parolee convictions for miscellaneous felony convictions *and* five violations of parole resulting in revocation by the board *without* court ordered recommitments—that is, to the C.Y.A. (data not shown). This finding deserves some

Table 5-5. Disposition by Severity of Offense: Most Serious Charge

	Severity of Offense							
	Discharges				Parolees			
	3-6		7-9		3-6		7-9	
Disposition	No.	%	No.	%	No.	%	No.	%
No conviction[a]	11	25.6	16	41.0	23	36.5	31	31.3
Miscellaneous conviction, other, fine only[b]	5	11.6	0	—	9	14.3	1	1.0
Probation	10	23.2	2	5.1	11	17.5	2	2.0
Jail 1-29 days	5	11.6	0	—	4	6.3	6	6.1
Jail 30-179 days	3	7.0	5	12.8	6	9.5	9	9.1
Jail 180+ days	5	11.6	9	23.1	5	7.9	24	24.2
C.Y.A.	3	7.0	5	12.8	4	6.3	7	7.1
Adult prison[c]	1	2.3	2	5.1	1	1.6	19	19.2
Total	43	100.0	39	100.0	63	100.0	99	100.0
Percentage convicted	63.5		68.7		74.4		59.0	

[a]Includes outstanding warrants, arrest, and release and dismissed at intake and at court.
[b]Includes suspended sentences, miscellaneous sentences (for example, restitution, work in the community), and death.
[c]Includes the California Department of Corrections, California Rehabilitation Center, out-of-state and federal prison commitments.
Note: Percentages may not add to 100.0 due to errors in rounding.

Table 5-6. Disposition of Charge Leading to Most Serious Disposition

	Discharges						Parolees					
	Person		Property		Drugs and other		Person		Property		Drugs and other	
Disposition	No.	%	No.	%	No.	%	No.	%	No.	%	No.	%
No conviction[a]	1	5.9	3	11.5	6	15.4	3	7.3	7	10.6	8	14.5
Miscellaneous conviction, other, fine only[b]	1	5.9	1	3.8	4	10.3	0	0.0	2	3.0	12	21.8
Probation	1	5.9	2	7.7	11	28.2	2	4.9	8	12.1	5	9.1
Jail 1-29 days	0	–	2	7.7	5	12.8	5	12.2	3	4.5	3	5.4
Jail 30-179 days	2	11.8	2	7.7	4	10.3	3	7.3	7	10.6	10	18.2
Jail 180+ days	5	29.4	8	30.8	4	10.3	6	14.6	17	25.8	4	7.3
C.Y.A.	4	23.5	4	15.4	1	2.6	4	9.8	11	16.7	7	12.7
Adult prison[c]	3	17.6	4	15.4	4	10.3	18	43.9	11	16.7	6	10.9
Total	17	100.0	26	100.0	39	100.0	41	100.0	66	100.0	55	100.0
Percentage convicted	94.1		88.5		84.6		92.7		89.4		85.4	

[a]Includes outstanding warrants, arrest, and release and dismissed at intake and at court.
[b]Includes suspended sentences, miscellaneous sentences (for example, restitution, work in the community), and death.
[c]Includes the California Department of Corrections, California Rehabilitation Center, out-of-state and federal prison commitments.
Note: Percentages may not add to 100.0 due to errors in rounding.

comment because it relates to the problem of spurious recidivism raised in Chapter 1. Are the overall results attributable to spurious recidivism? Three of the revocations were for robbery, petty theft, and burglary, respectively, among individuals who had already received local sentences of between seven months and one year. In one remaining case there was no local commitment for a charge of auto theft and the case resulted in C.Y.A. recommitment for a technical. In the final case a parolee was not convicted of a drug-related charge but admitted heroin use and had his parole revoked, resulting in a two-month C.Y.A. stay. If an adjustment is made for the fact of revocation rather than court recommitment to the C.Y.A. (by removing these cases), the finding of no difference in relative percentages returned to the C.Y.A. by court orders is maintained. These data, then, indicate that in this context spurious recidivism does not raise serious problems of interpretation so far as conviction data are concerned.

Nor do they appear to seriously inflate custody data. With two exceptions revocations resulting in C.Y.A. commitments merely substituted C.Y.A. for county jail time. Both the robbery and burglary revocations resulted in commitments to the C.Y.A. that were within one week of the court-imposed length of sentence to county jail. In the third case (petty theft) the time spent in C.Y.A. was actually 35 days less than the original jail sentence, although reliable information on adjudicative detention in the C.Y.A. was not available for this individual. Assuming this lasted no longer than one month, the time spent in C.Y.A. was approximately what it would have been had the parolee spent time in county jail, providing he was not released on county jail parole, which is not extensively used but is unreported on rap sheets.

The remaining two youths spent time in custody that may not have occurred had the individual not been on parole (spurious custody time). For the parole violation involving drugs this resulted in two months time, as noted above. The violation for auto theft is not so clear but is certainly revealing: the parolee was returned to an institution on a technical violation and escaped two and one-half months later; he was then actually charged with escape and spent time in county jail pending trial and eventually returned to the C.Y.A. as a court recommitment for misdemeanor escape. The individual then spent an additional seven and one-half months in institutions before release to parole.

A conservative estimate of the extra time spent by the parolees whose most serious disposition involved the C.Y.A. is about four and one-half months, and at most slightly less than a year.

When time spent in institutions for parole violations involving technicals is added to time spent in temporary detention, the minimum amount of extra time spent due to parole was about 8.2 months.[2] Seven individuals spent a total of 113 days in temporary detention for an average of 16 days each. A liberal estimate of extra time spent is therefore about 15.7 months. These data suggest that the amount of spurious custody time is not great enough to question findings that the two groups differ in place of institutionalization and that there is no overall difference in time spent in custody. They also do not appear to affect findings relating to differentials in adult prison time.

Disposition by Severity of Charge

As shown in Table 5-7, high severity parolee charges, including scores of 7, 8, and 9, were more likely to receive adult prison sentences while the discharges were more likely to receive C.Y.A. and jail sentences of 180 days or more.[3] For low severity charges of 2 and 3, the discharges were 3.4 times more likely to receive probation than the parolees, reflecting the drug- and alcohol-related dispositions.

Moderately severe charges (4, 5, and 6) show the parolees receiving a greater percentage of probation sentences and the discharges a higher percentage of heavy jail sentences.

To summarize: the parolees received more punitive court-imposed penalties per offense than the discharges. This finding holds when controlling for the nature or severity of offense. The pattern is most obvious in sentences for personal crimes, where the parolees exceed the discharges in sentences to adult prison when charges of homicide and rape are excluded from the analysis. It is also found for drug- and alcohol-related charges or low to moderate severity scores. In both comparisons the parolees were sentenced to more jail and the discharges to more probation. These data appear to indicate that a parole status provokes a greater amount of punishment than that given to a comparable group of individuals not on parole.

The general convergence of the results when using the two methods suggests there are genuine differences in sentences. Both suggest that sentences were not simply a function of the nature or severity of charges. Thus the question to be investigated is whether differences in sentences can be explained on grounds other than the absence of a parole status. After briefly reviewing the characteristics of those receiving various dispositions, this question will be examined.

Dispositions by Background Characteristics

Black parolees were far more likely to receive prison sentences than the black discharges—the latter, in contrast, were more likely to receive probation, particularly for drug- and alcohol-related offenses. The black parolees were more often charged with offenses of higher severity; in fact, in terms of rank, black parolees had the highest mean severity scores (5.8), white and black discharges followed (5.3), and white parolees had the lowest (5.0). The only significant difference in scores, as shown in Table 5-8, is between black and white parolees. But it was also true that the black parolees were more likely to be convicted of violent personal and property crimes.

Table 5-7. Disposition by Severity of Charge: Most Serious Disposition

	Severity of Offense											
	Discharges						Parolees					
	2-3		4-6		7-9		2-3		4-6		7-9	
Disposition	No.	%	No.	%	No.	%	No.	%	No.	%	No.	%
No conviction[a]	5	19.2	4	12.9	2	8.0	6	18.8	9	14.3	3	4.5
Miscellaneous conviction, other fine only[b]	2	7.7	3	9.7	0	0.0	9	28.1	4	6.3	1	1.5
Probation	11	42.3	3	9.7	0	0.0	4	12.5	9	14.3	2	3.0
Jail 1-29 days	4	15.4	3	9.7	0	0.0	2	6.2	6	9.5	3	4.5
Jail 30-179 days	0	0.0	4	12.9	4	16.0	6	18.8	11	17.5	3	4.5
Jail 180+ days	2	7.7	7	22.6	8	32.0	2	6.2	6	9.5	19	28.4
C.Y.A.	0	0.0	4	12.9	5	20.0	2	6.2	12	19.0	8	11.9
Adult prison[c]	2	7.7	3	9.7	6	24.0	1	3.1	6	9.5	28	41.8
Total	26	100.0	31	100.0	25	100.0	32	100.0	63	100.0	67	100.0
Percentage convicted	80.8		90.3		92.0		81.2		85.7		95.5	

[a]Includes outstanding warrants, arrest, and release and dismissed at intake and at court.
[b]Includes suspended sentences, miscellaneous sentences (for example, restitution, work in the community), and death.
[c]Includes the California Department of Corrections, California Rehabilitation Center, out-of-state and federal prison commitments.
Note: Percentages may not add to 100.0 due to errors in rounding.

Table 5-8. Severity of Offense by Race

Race	Discharges			Parolees			
	Mean	S.D.	No.	Mean	S.D.	No.	t
Whites	5.3	1.7	25	5.0	1.7	56	.72[a]
Blacks	5.3	1.9	47	5.8	1.7	90	1.62[b]

[a]$p < .20$, df = 79. The difference between black and white parolees is significant, $t = 2.9, p < .01$, df = 144.
[b]$p < .10$, df = 135.

In part the more serious dispositions for black parolees emanated from these differences in offense. They appear to have resulted from the more severe charges of the parolees in general and blacks in particular when controlling for age: black parolee charges *increased* in severity as age increased, while mean scores for the black discharges *decreased*. Discharges 18 years of age or less had mean severity scores of 5.9, the parolees 5.6; for those 21 years of age and over the discharge mean is 4.8, the parolees', 5.6 (see Table 5-9; data for blacks are not shown). And when dispositions are crossclassified by age the importance of the latter becomes clearer: 30 percent of the blacks 21 years of age and older were sentenced to adult prison while only 15 percent of the discharges were (data not shown). It seems reasonable to assume that sentencing alternatives decrease when the age at commission of offenses, particularly serious ones, is above that necessary for recommitment to the C.Y.A. Official categories or demographic characteristics, in other words, may have real consequences for sentencing.

Table 5-9. Severity of Charges by Age

Age Category	Discharges			Parolees			
	Mean	S.D.	No.	Mean	S.D.	No.	t
18 or less	5.9	1.6	22	5.6	1.8	26	0.7[a]
19-20	4.9	1.8	33	5.4	1.9	65	1.4[b]
21 and over	4.8	1.9	27	5.6	1.8	71	1.8[c]

[a]$p < .20$, df = 46.
[b]$p < .20$, df = 96.
[c]$p < .10$, df = 96.

Given the small number of cases in the study it is difficult to disentangle the possible confounding effects of other factors which may influence disposition outcomes, particularly when using crosstabular analysis. Even though race, nature or severity of offense, experimental status, and age are related to adult prison sentences, still another significant predictor of this disposition is the amount of prior time spent on parole as of March 1, 1976. Parolees with 7 to 18 months prior parole at the start of the study were more likely than the discharges to receive an adult prison sentence. Discharges in this category received slightly more probation and jail of 180 days or more, which makes sense given that they were charged with more drug- and alcohol-related offenses than the parolees. And to complicate matters more, parolee property offenders and those spending 13 or more months in institutions before release to parole were more likely to receive an adult prison sentence, even though there were no a priori differences between the two groups in this category (data not shown).

These complexities suggest that what is needed is a multivariate approach to the question of what accounts for disparities. Available methods, such as logistic regression (LOGIT) or ordinary least squares estimation (OLS), enable one to examine the relationship between a dichotomous dependent variable and categorical and interval independent variables. There is currently some controversy over the use of OLS estimates but these criticisms do not preclude its exploratory use here.[4]

At present our attention focuses on convictions for the charge leading to the most serious disposition. This method is chosen because it is the most conservative approach: disparities in sentencing are of a lesser magnitude than found for the most serious charge. The models are not meant to describe all of the factors related to sentencing, only those which in bivariate form were found to be associated with either being charged with a personal crime or a sentence to adult prison.

The primary question in this analysis is: to what extent do race, age, commitment offense, etc., *directly* affect sentencing to adult prison and to what extent do they *indirectly* affect sentencing through the fact of being convicted of a personal offense? A secondary question is whether the bivariate relationships are spurious; that is, due to colinearity or multicolinearity among the independent variables.

For purposes of analysis all of the variables in this additive regression equation are "dummy coded" (1 or 0), as shown below:

S = prison sentence: (1)/no prison sentence (0)

C = current personal offense: (1)/no current personal offense (0)

A = age 21 and over at 3/1/76: (1)/not age 21 and over at 3/1/76 (0)

P = prior parole months: 7-18 (1)/not prior parole months 7-18 (0)

R = race black: (1)/race not black (0)

$\emptyset$ = commitment offense property-related (1)/commitment offense not property-related (0)

I = prior institution time 13 or more months (1)/prior institution time not 13 or more months (0).

The regression equation takes the form:

$$S = a + b_1 C + b_2 A + b_3 P + b_4 R + b_5 \wp + b_6 I + e$$

where "a" is the constant or intercept, b_1, b_2, b_3 ... b_6 represent unstandardized b coefficients and "e" the error or residual variation in S which is unexplained by the independent variables included in the equation. The b coefficients represent marginal changes in the probability of S while controlling for all other variables in the equation. The constant term is the point where the regression line crosses the Y axis.

The analysis was performed by computing a common regression equation. This required that each independent variable be multiplied by experimental status (coded 1 if discharged from parole and 0 if not), resulting in six interaction terms. The regression itself was conducted in two steps: first the main effects (b_1 through b_6) were entered; and then the interaction terms were added. An F-test was then performed to determine whether the increment in R^2 due to the addition of the interaction terms significantly increased the R^2.

The mean scores for the variables in the equation can be found in Table 5-10. Four regression models (two each for the discharges and parolees), the b coefficients and significance levels are presented in Table 5-11. Model I includes personal offense conviction in the equation while Model II excludes it. By subtracting the b's of Model I from Model II, estimates can be made of the direct effects of the independent variables and a parole status on S apart from their indirect influence through conviction of a personal offense (C).

The results show that race, age, prior institution time of 13 or more months, and age 21 or over have both direct and indirect effects on the probability of sentence, but only for the parolees. For the parolees the influence of a property-related commitment offense is entirely indirect. The significant coefficients for the discharges indicate that the slopes differ from those of the parolees (because of this the intercepts are not readily interpretable). This reflects the significant increase in R^2 due to the addition of the interaction terms to the equation. It is clear that conviction of a personal offense is important in predicting only the parolees' marginal probability of sentence to prison. But more important is the finding that the relationship of age, race, prior parole, and prior institution time with S is not due solely to each of their effects on the likelihood of being convicted of a personal crime. In addition, the simple fact that youth in these categories are on parole appears to directly affect their increased probability of sentence to prison.[5]

The equations can also be used to predict the probability of S for each group with and without current offense in the equation. By multiplying the separate sample means for each variable times the respective b coefficients, the predicted S for the parolees (.304) is almost two times greater than that of the discharges (.153). When current offense is excluded the respective predictions are .219 and .149.

**Table 5-10. Means and Standard Deviations
for Variables in the Regression Equation**

Variable	Mean	S.D.
S	.213	.410
C	.250	.434
A	.417	.494
P	.370	.484
B	.551	.499
∅	.537	.500
I	.232	.423

**Table 5-11. Regression of Prison Sentence (S) on Current Offense
and Background Factors (Model I) and Background
Factors Only (Model II)**

Variable	Model I		Model II		Direct Effects	
	Discharge	Parolee	Discharge	Parolee	Discharge	Parolee
C	.05	.28**	—[a]	—[a]		
A	.04	.12*	.04	.12*	.00	.01[d]
P	−.25**[b]	.06	−.25**[b]	.08	.00	.02
B	−.02	.14**	−.02	.18**	.00	.03[d]
I	.00	.15*	−.01	.18**	.00	.03
∅	−.15**	.14**	−.15**	.14**	.00	.00
Intercept	.29[c]	−.10[c]	.30[c]	−.05[c]		
Overall F	3.6**		2.7**			
Adjusted R^2	.14		.08			
R^2 increment	.06		.05			
F-value for increment	3.27		3.43			

*$p < .05$
**$p < .10$
[a]Model II excludes C from the equation (see text).
[b]Discharge and parolee slopes differ significantly.
[c]Intercept differences are not readily interpretable because there are slope differences.
[d]The direct effects of race and age do not subtract correctly here due to errors in rounding.

Overall, the results indicate that a parole status appears to act as a penalty, particularly among those who are older, with a moderate amount of prior parole as of March 1, 1976, who are black, and who spent 13 or more months in institutions before release to parole. There is, therefore, a disparity in the extent to which the "punishment fits the crime," which can be explained in part by the fact of being on parole. The more serious sentences of the parolees cannot be explained solely by the fact of their more serious charges.

CHAPTER SUMMARY

The data presented in this chapter suggest that a parole status may be relevant at the point of sanctioning in the justice process. Its effects are shown in the greater likelihood of more serious sentences for parolees charged with personal crimes or more severe charges and the greater likelihood of discharges to receive probation for drug- and alcohol-related offenses. It is particularly evident among certain categories of parolees: older blacks with a moderate amount of prior parole who spent more time in institutions before release. Moreover, parolees charged with personal offenses do worse in terms of seriousness of sentence after both current offense and selected background characteristics have been controlled for. Interpretations of these findings and those presented earlier can be found in the next chapter.

NOTES

1. Researchers typically examine custody-*free* time rather than time spent *in* custody. The two outcomes are, of course, equivalent in meaning insamuch as either can be taken to imply time spent both in and out of custody. This study has used time *in* custody in order to more clearly show how differential reactions at the point of sentencing may have resulted in disparate patterns of sentencing in the criminal justice system.

2. This figure would probably be higher if we had data on the amount of detention of parolees in local facilities; since the parole files were destroyed the data are not available. Moreover, the number of detentions could well have been higher if the study had been located closer to the Northern Reception Center Clinic, given the cost of local detention.

3. I restrict attention from here to the end of the chapter to the charge resulting in the most serious disposition, for reasons noted in the text.

4. The models developed here generally meet the four criteria mentioned by Goodman (1975, p. 18) for comparable results using alternative methods.

5. The results do not change substantially when controlling for base expectancy score and prior record of contacts and commtiments.

6
Social
Control Interpreted:
The Paradox at Work

The findings of Chapter 3 are congruent with the prevailing opinion that attempts to rehabilitate and control offenders do not have their intended effects. These findings and those of Chapter 5 also suggest a negative effect: a parole status may result in more serious types of offenses among certain categories of offenders and then amplify the penalties for the crimes at the point of sentencing.

This chapter places these results in the context of debates concerned with social control (in particular, theories of labeling and deterrence), interprets differences in the nature and severity of charges and provides materials for understanding sentencing differentials.

PAROLE AS A DETERRENT?

As noted in Chapter 1, Sacks and Logan (1979) have argued that parole acts as a deterrent. This effect is said to stem from the reporting and surveillance requirements of parole and to the restraining impact of an "overhanging sentence," the mainstay of the indeterminate sentence and parole. In the literature on deterrence, parole is often assumed to be a deterrent (see Stanley, 1976; Lerner, 1977; Martinson and Wilks, 1977; but see Gibbs, 1975, pp. 65-67), although it is unclear whether deterrence will have its intended effects on all "marginal groups" in society—that is, individuals who may be considered likely to engage in criminal acts (Zimring and Hawkins, 1968). Zimring and Hawkins (1973), in fact, suggest that some individuals are insulated from threats of punishment: "According to Lewin, among those who do *not* respect 'the ideology, that is, the moral limitations of the group, threats of punishment frequently become ineffective' because 'exclusion from the group' is not seen as a significant penalty" (p. 193). And Glaser (1971) suggests that some individuals may have a 'stake in *non*conformity" and will react to labeling by drift toward secondary deviation.

The central question, therefore, concerns the conditions under which labeling or deterrence, or both, or neither, will occur. Some theorists have argued that deterrence is more or less effective depending upon the seriousness of the offense in question. One such statement is made by Morris (1951, p. 13): "the effectiveness of deterrence varies in inverse proportion to the moral seriousness of the crime" (cf. Zimring, 1971, pp. 44-45; quoted in Waldo and Chiricos, 1972). The assumption here is that passive social control inhibits or restrains the individual from committing more serious crimes but that less serious behavior, such as smoking marijuana[1] or premarital sex[2] may require active social control for their containment or restraint.

An alternative statement is made by Chambliss (1967), who draws a distinction between *instrumental* acts, ones oriented to "the attainment of some other goal," and *expressive* acts, which are "committed because [they are] pleasurable in and of [themselves] and not because [they are] a route to some other goal." Expressive crimes are, like more serious offenses in the statement of Morris, resistant to the threat of punishment. Instrumental acts, in contrast, are not. There does not appear to be an implicit gradation of seriousness in this theory, since expressive crimes can include both murder and drug addiction and instrumental crimes both shoplifting and professional burglary. Instead, *within* these broad classes of criminal acts, penalties will be more or less effective depending upon the extent to which an individual is committed to crime as a way of life. Overall, though, instrumental offenses are seen as most susceptible to deterrence and expressive crimes the least (see page 713, where the likelihood of deterrence is rank ordered). In no case, however, is the prediction made that sanctioning may result in an *increase* in level of seriousness of certain offenses.

The present data are inconsistent with the deterrence hypothesis of Chambliss (1967) predicting fewer "instrumental" acts and at least no difference in "expressive" acts. The significantly greater percentages of arrest and conviction for property offenses among older parolees and the differences in favor of the discharges for homicide and rape appear to contradict this thesis. Moreover, the greater percentage of drug- and alcohol-related offenses among the discharges, when viewed in conjunction with the homicide and rape charges, suggests in general that the theory does not go far enough in predicting that social control will result in a decrease in less serious expressive crimes. The exception may be charges for battery which, like those for burglary, an instrumental offense, are less consistent across methods in the present data. In any case, it appears that for this group of offenders, parole may *exacerbate* the seriousness of crime.

Based on the statement of Morris one would at least expect no difference between the two groups in the incidence of more serious crimes of homicide and rape and a reduction of less serious parolee crimes. The net result would be an overall reduction in crime. As shown in Chapter 3, however, the data reveal no overall difference in percentage arrested and convicted, only differences in the nature and severity of offenses. The greater percentage of property offenses among older parolees and of serious personal crimes appears to directly contradict the theory, as was the case with Chambliss. Moreover, the significantly higher severity of parolee charges questions the thesis. The only support for the argument of Morris is the greater percentage of less severe drug- and alcohol-related offenses brought against the discharges.

Perhaps the most significant finding related to deterrence theory is that social control may maintain or alter the choice-making behavior of individuals *but not necessarily toward conventional pursuits.* Evidence presented earlier indicates that active social control merely alters its form in such a way that it becomes relatively more serious and secondary in nature.

Why does the deterrence argument fail to explain these findings? In general, these data question the extent to which deterrence theory applies to individuals who have already been stigmatized through conviction, incarceration, and ostensibly parole. Zimring and Hawkins (1973, p. 193) argue as much:

> . . . when an offender has been stigmatized once, the effects of this
> process are likely to stay with him for many years . . . the offender
> will have less incentive to avoid further consequences that bring with
> them the threat of stigma.

The present data suggest that the lesser "incentive to avoid further consequences," like Studt's (1967, p. 3-4) observation that parole may lead to "either low commitment or habitual flirting with danger," and Glaser's that some individuals develop a "stake in *non*conformity," is maintained or reinforced by a parole status.

How this process occurs deserves some comment. It may be that the parole status modified choice making at the individual level by providing alternative structural contexts in which drift toward more serious criminal activity could occur. It could also be that the parole status maintained preexisting tendencies to commit more serious crimes—that is, by preventing maturational reform. The two processes may interact: maturational reform is impeded through channeling of behavior toward more serious crime. There is some evidence, for example, that a parole officer's intervention may merely change the type of crime the parolee commits:

> One time I was arrested on an assault charge and the police called
> my parole officer. When he showed up, he told me to stay away
> from personal crimes or he would violate me. So I started doing
> burglaries—I thought it was kind of strange, but it was like he didn't
> mind knowing I was doing burglaries as long as I didn't hurt anyone.
> (Petersilia, Greenwood, and Lavin, 1977, p. 51)

Of course in this example the move is from personal to property-related crimes, while the present data suggest that the move is from drug and alcohol toward more serious personal or property crimes. The reason may be that, due to the visible nature of drug- and alcohol-related crimes and the possibility of their detection by parole agents, those retained on parole were less likely to be charged with these offenses. Instead they gravitated toward more serious property and personal crimes.[3]

Irwin (1970, p. 90) suggests additional factors related to parolee perceptions and agent practices which may lead to "blowing up" and perhaps more explosive crimes. He notes that the "belief in his own strong proclivity towards deviance is an important aspect in the thought processes of the criminal. He believes that statistically the chances are strong that he will return to deviance . . . the prisoner often takes the view that any difficulty or unusual circumstances might divert him towards the old bag, and that once pointed in that direction it is difficult to change course." One such circumstance is that of an "intolerant" parole agent who attempts to penetrate deeply into the parolee's life:

> Perceived intolerance in the agent's orientation [which includes agents with the "social worker" orientation to parole, who in practice are more punitive in orientation than "cop-oriented" agents, due to their class and cultural backgrounds] requires the maintenance of greater distance and more deceit. Intolerance coupled with intensity puts the parolee in the most difficult position. If any [agent/parolee] equilibrium is to be maintained, he must reduce his deviant activities greatly, which may greatly curtail and/or obstruct his pleasurable, satisfying, or meaningful experiences and relationships. This in turn may lead to his "blowing up."

While these studies provide an explanation for parolee tendencies toward criminal behavior in general, they do not specify factors that account for offense differences found here. One may speculate that this choice was affected by the means of social control, which perhaps unintentionally legitimizes the commission of crimes against others. Henry and Short (1954, pp. 102-103), whose discussion is not examined in detail here, note that "when behavior is required to conform rigidly to the demands and expectations of others . . . the expression of aggression against others is legitimized." It may be that the stringent behavioral expectations of a parolee, which constitute an important dimension of the theory on which the authority of parole rests, provide a symbolic medium through which the parolee can justify or legitimize crimes against society. In contrast, when individuals are not on parole, "when behavior is freed from external restraint, the self must bear the responsibility for frustration," which in this case takes the form of more self-destructive drug and alcohol violations. This explanation implies, however, a constant motivation or tendency to commit crimes across experimental groups, presumably ensured by randomization. Nonetheless, the question of how drift toward more serious crime occurs is in need of further research.

These points, taken together, imply that some consideration must be given to the notion that a parole status may be neither an act of grace nor a status passage (Studt, 1967). Waller (1972) correctly points out that to equate parole with a status passage implies an elevation in status, which does not stand up in the data presented here. It may be that discharge from parole is a necessary but hardly a sufficient condition for resisting more serious crime.

OFFICIAL CATEGORIZATIONS AND SENTENCING

Kitsuse and Cicourel (1963) and McCleary (1978) have argued that official statistics should be viewed as organizational products and interpreted solely as outcomes of inter- and intraorganizational processes. Strange as it may sound, one can detect an implicit official bias in these views. For example, McCleary (1978, p. 150) argues that one consequence of inadequate parole records (ones which do not accurately describe the actual behavior of parolees) is that classification and processing of them is done in a "total information vacuum." This "suggests that the [Department of Corrections] makes no decisions of any consequence."

The argument seems to presuppose that parole officials could make the "right" decisions if they had good parole records or, more importantly, that the decision can only be of "consequence" if it is based on "all the facts." One practical import of this view could be that agents, if they can, should collect better information and only then can the "right" decisions—with consequences— be made.

What these views neglect is that official crime is at a minimum a product of both individual behavior *and* organizational reaction to crime. As argued in Chapter 1, it is important to understand the role of organizational generation of spurious recidivism, particularly at the level of arrest but also at the level of disposition. As shown in Chapter 4, evidence suggests that arrest data in particular were not likely a spurious artifact of social control based on parole status. However, Chapter 5 suggested that there was differential reaction based on parole status at the level of disposition.

For the present discussion, then, the most serious deficiency of these views is that they radically detach the activities of officials from the behavior of individuals they collect statistics on and, in turn, obviate the possibility of understanding the consequences of social control. To argue that official statistics or parolee outcomes reflect the activities of officials—and leave it at that—neglects the consequences of organizational processing, classification, stereotyping, and bureaucratization for individuals (see Schwartz and Skolnick, 1970). The main point here, then, is that official categorizations, such as parole status, may have important consequences.

Disposition Patterns

The data on dispositions of offenses for the most serious charge presented in Chapter 5 provide an interesting contrast with Star's (1979) finding that California Department of Corrections summary parolees were returned to prison an equal percentage of the time as those given regular parole supervision—only through a different administrative route (through court versus revocation of parole). The data in this study show that the overall percentage of the two groups sentenced to relatively more lengthy state and local lockup (including jail 180 days or over, C.Y.A., and adult prison) is quite similar, but that the parolees received commitments to adult prison more often than did the discharges. The difference in dispositional patterns reflects the unique structural niche of youthful offenders, the nature of the offenses of the parolees, and selection due to a parole status. The difference in sentences can not be directly linked with board action: there were no referrals to the C.Y.A. which were refused and returned to court for alternative sentencing. The latter practice of the C.Y.A., that of rejecting potential commitments, was of obvious concern to some, however. In one case a parolee had been convicted of both burglary and robbery and sentenced to the C.Y.A. His attorney asked the judge if the young man could have concurrent sentences if the C.Y.A. should return him as "unfit" for commitment and he should be sentenced to the penitentiary. The judge replied that he would not necessarily send him there, but that if he did the sentence would run concurrently.

In an unknown number of other cases commitment to a state institution is contingent upon whether the youth has a job, simplistic as this may sound. One judge, in considering whether to sentence a young male convicted of grand theft auto to the C.Y.A., flatly stated that "my practice is if you have a job and you are acceptable to Work Furlough, I put you in Work Furlough rather than throw you out of your job. But if Work Furlough says they won't take you, that means you can do time. I just can't help it."[4] The ward was eventually committed to the C.Y.A. Thus, the sources of sentencing differentials are extremely complex. The broad discretion that may be exercised after conviction may provide a fertile ground for decisions to be made on particularistic grounds, such as that relating to parole status.

Organizational Sources of Sentencing Patterns

Inspection of case files and observations gathered on field visits both at the parole units and court suggest some additional reasons for differentials in sentencing. Four items will be explored here: 1. the role of official supervisory categorizations of parolees in the choice of sentencing dispositions; 2. communication and cooperation between probation and parole, a long-standing practice; 3. the definition of a parole status as one of aggravation; and 4. detention and case processing in the plea bargaining process.

The Role of Official Categorizations: Probation, Parole and
Overlapping Supervision

Case files and court records of individuals sentenced to the C.Y.A., adult prison, and community alternatives were examined to locate possible reasons for sentencing differentials. One probation officer's presentence investigation reviewed a parolee's case history and recommended institutionalization. His choice of an institutional disposition appeared hinged on awareness of the parolee's supervision on both probation *and* parole. He wrote:

> Since any form of noninstitutional disposition would needlessly
> duplicate [supervisory] services, I faithfully recommend commit-
> ment to the Department of Corrections.[5]

Parole, he argued, had not worked, nor had probation, and community alternatives had been exhausted. Further supervision would "needlessly dupli-cate services."

If this assumption were applied on a system-wide basis, and there is reason to believe it is not (discussed below), the argument could be made that the dis-charges have been given an advantage at the point of sentencing. Having shed one form of supervision—parole—the discharge would by definition have more alternatives other than institutionalization. Can it be argued on these grounds that the lack of a parole status results in more lenient treatment by the court?

The data suggest the answer is "no" and that there is little concern with the costs of duplicate services. First of all, approximately equal percentages of the two groups were on probation at the time of the study starting date, including 12 percent of the discharges and 17 percent of the parolees (see Table 6-1). About 4 percent of the discharges and 9 percent of the parolees had been on probation for six months prior to the starting date. Between 8 percent and 9 percent of both groups had been on probation between 7 and 30 months prior to the start of the study. Since the two groups had a similar history of probation at the time the study began it was not a likely influence on the findings.

Second, if probation sentences are meted out in light of other supervisory statuses, one would expect two findings: 1. the discharges would be granted probation at an earlier point in the study follow-up and to a greater extent than would the parolees; one might roughly refer to this as taking up the criminal justice process "slack"; and 2. the amount of time spent on probation would be greater for the discharges. To test these hypotheses both the timing of pro-bation sentences and the amount of time spent on probation during the follow-up period were calculated on the basis of probation sentences for *all* convictions. Some probation sentences did not show up in prior tables because only one (the most serious) disposition was included in them.

The two groups do not differ greatly in overall mean time to probation sentences, as measured in months, nor do they differ in time to probation sen-tences among those who received probation. Overall, as shown in Table 6-2, the

Table 6-1. Number and Percentage on Probation at March 1, 1976,
by Month Placed on Probation

Probation status	Discharges		Parolees	
	No.	%	No.	%
Total on probation	12	12.2	34	17.2
Prior month placed on probation (pre-March 1, 1976				
1-6 past months	4	4.1	17	8.6
7-30 past months	8	8.2	17	8.6
Not on probation	86	87.8	164	82.8
Total cases	98	100.0	198	100.0

parolees received probation sentences slightly sooner than the discharges: the parolee mean number of months to first probation sentence imposed during the follow-up is 5.4, and for the discharges it is 6.5, which is not a statistically significant difference. Among those receiving probation sentences the discharges took 13.5 months to their first probation sentence, and the parolees 14.0 months. The discharges were more likely to receive probation at 10 to 12 months into the study period (X^2 = 6.3, $p < .02$; data not shown), but the number of cases is very small. The trend is also not strong enough to produce statistical significance among those who received a probation sentence. These data suggest that there is no difference in the timing of probation sentences.

Table 6-2. Months to Probation Sentences

Months to probation	Discharges	Parolees
Overall mean	6.5	5.4
S.D.	8.0	7.5
Mean per case	13.5	13.9
No.	47	76

The hypothesis predicting differential amounts of time on probation for the two groups is also not supported, as shown in Table 6-3. Altogether 48 percent of the discharges and 38 percent of the parolees received one or more probation sentences during the follow-up, a modest difference. However, both

Table 6-3. Months on Probation during 26-Month Follow-up

Months on probation	Discharges		Parolees	
	No.	%	No.	%
1-6 months	8	17.0	7	9.2
7-12 months	15	31.9	17	22.4
13-18 months	8	17.0	31	40.8
19-26 months	16	34.0	21	27.6
Total	47	100.0	76	100.0
Overall mean		6.76		5.5[a]
S.D.		7.05		6.5
No.		98		198
Mean per case		14.1		14.4[a]
S.D.		7.0		5.7
No.		47		122

[a]t-test not significant.

Note: Percentages may not add to 100.0 due to errors in rounding.

groups actually spent an equal amount of time per case receiving probation during the study period (discharge mean = 14.1; parolee mean = 14.4). These findings therefore do not support the hypothesis that leniency or the lack of it was due to the simple fact of being officially under the supervisory status of parole. The difference in probation sentences is at least in part due to differing offenses of the two groups.

Other data, in fact, suggest that the practice of "duplicate supervision" of parole and probation is widespread. Fully 37 percent of the parolees were on both parole and probation for at least one month during the 26-month follow-up (see Table 6-4). The overall mean number of months spent on probation and parole was 4.1 months, while the mean number of months spent on both probation and parole for individuals on both forms of supervision at any time during the study period was 11.0.

Given that about 73 percent of the parolees were discharged during the follow-up period, a correction should be made for the amount of overlapping supervision among parolees who *could* have experienced dual supervision. Over the entire study period the parolees spent 3,049 months on parole. In addition to these months on parole, 803 were also spent on probation: a little over 26 percent of the total amount of time spent on parole was also spent on probation (data not shown).

These periods of dual supervision were not necessarily brief. For example, 19 percent of the parolees on probation and parole—7 percent of all the parolees —spent between 19 and 26 months of the follow-up period on dual supervision; 16 percent spent between 13 and 18 months.

Table 6-4. Overlapping Months on Parole and Probation Supervision

Supervision status	Parolees only	
	No.	%
Total on probation and parole	73	100.0
Months of overlapping supervision		
1-6 months	26	35.6
7-12 months	21	28.8
13-18 months	12	16.4
19-26 months	14	19.2
Sum	803	
Overall mean	4.06	
S.D.	7.05	
Mean per case	11.0	
S.D.	7.5	

There may be important implications of dual jurisdictional controls for the parolee. In a blatant violation of the rule of "no dual supervision," a judge, at the time of sentence of a parolee to the C.Y.A. for burglary, ordered that probation for the offense be terminated when the ward was released to parole in order to avoid duplication. However, the parolee was also convicted of forgery and placed on felony probation *at the same time* so that the judge could commit him to state prison for violation of probation, "if that [were] necessary," *after* his release from institutionalization.[6] What the effects of the imposition of dual controls of this kind are on the individual is a matter of speculation. What if probation and parole rules conflict or overlap? Who shall assume responsibility for the parolee? To what extent do dual controls interfere or conflict with any progress made during a C.Y.A. institution and parole stay?

Communication Between Probation and Parole

As Smith (1949, pp. 70-83) wrote about the C.Y.A. some time ago, parole is "an important source of unanticipated consequences for the Authority.... As a functioning member of a community, the parole officer incurs obligations to the community he serves, even though these ... may be unintentional. It is at this level that field policy can be formulated." One such instance of unanticipated consequences is that which grows from cooperation between probation and parole.[7] The board dictates that it has power to make ultimate C.Y.A. dispositions, as indeed it does; but in everyday practice parole agents have considerable input into court dispositions, largely as influence directed through the probation officer, but is more applicable to adult than juvenile cases. In Alameda county, Assembly Bill 3121 (AB 3121), passed in 1976, was interpreted to mean that the probation officer relinquished responsibility for filing petitions to the prosecutor. Before AB 3121, the Director of the C.Y.A. ordered that decisions to file juvenile petitions be made by court appointed officials; after AB 3121, what few requests were made by the court to the C.Y.A. parole officers for recommendations on juvenile petitions dropped to almost none in Alameda county, and to a lesser extent in Contra Costa county. The general practice, though, particularly for adults, is a consequence of agency policy to cooperate with criminal justice officials, especially probation officials.

Parole agent input into the justice process is particularly evident in presentence reports. Probation officers, in part to save time, rely on parole agents to supply information on the current family and job situation of a ward, general progress on parole, and the status of the youth in the C.Y.A. However, one agent felt that the best point at which to influence the disposition of a case in a positive way was before the actual pretrial hearing:

> If we can get into it before pretrial we have a much better chance
> of influencing the sentence. We can get a shorter sentence by
> coming up with an alternative plan to deal with the ward that
> the judge will buy. The judge is the most stable person of the
> whole bunch and I prefer talking to him. It doesn't matter if
> it is a felony or not if it makes sense to the judge. This is a way
> we can help.[8]

Agents are noticeably reluctant to forecast C.Y.A. board dispositions, however. One unit supervisor, while admitting that agents occasionally forecast what action will probably be taken with a case by the C.Y.A. parole board, stated that "We don't know for certain what the Board will do with a case. We know pretty well what certain Board members will do, but we don't know who will judge on the case. So we can't make any promises."[9]

Nonetheless, parole agents can indirectly influence the disposition of a case through the provision of information to probation officers. For adult cases this practice is sometimes formalized with a blank form for the parole officer to fill out. In some cases requests for recommendations as to dispositions are regulated by a quick calculation of time remaining in jurisdiction, other things being equal. One probation officer tried out his recommendation to adult prison for a parolee convicted of several counts of forgery in order to elicit the agent's response. The agent looked at time remaining in C.Y.A. jurisdiction, which was six months—too short for another incarceration-parole loop—and said, "Don't send him back to us. We don't want him."[10] In many other cases, including the bulk of less serious offenses, agents "explain the situation" and offer a recommendation to the probation officer. Agents sometimes interpret this practice as allowing them to "play God." One said "It gives us a sense of power in the little niche we work, like we're omnipotent. Some agents really get into that feeling and play it up."[11] Some agents, but not all, claim that the probation officers follow their recommendations in almost every such case unless there is widely disparate input from other sources. There are no hard data in the present study to support this claim, but it appears tenable.

This practice does not, of course, directly go against board powers since a disposition is not promised. But the informal and formal process is maintained by parole board policy to wait until most court dispositions have been made before acting on parole violations, which may be more typical for adults than for juveniles. This gap in the system allows parole officers to affect both court and eventual board dispositions, but not to determine either. The hiatus, incidentally, also gives rise to the parole agent question of "who they serve"—the public, the board, the parolee, themselves—during the course of after-arrest events. The issue also raised the question of whether agents use their discretionary powers solely to "save a parolee." McCleary (1978, p. 80) appears to have made this argument, as shown in his statement that the discretionary power of agents "is the power to 'save' a client by holding out for a bargain that will not affect the client's status as a parolee." Even though agents in his study participated directly in the plea bargaining process, his own observations do not appear to support the statement. One parole officer stated, for example:

> . . . I don't make distinctions between guilty and innocent men.
> I'll help a guilty man beat a rap if I can and if he deserves a break,
> and I'll watch an innocent man go down the tubes if I have to.
> (pp. 83-84)

Some agents in the present study admitted as much. One flatly stated that "We repeat the pattern of rejection. We turn our back on them sometimes. If a ward doesn't get along with his agent this supervisor may insist that the agent go out and see him and see how he's doing. One result is that the agent may slant reports the other way [against the parolee] ."[12] Another agent made reference to the situation of somewhat older parolees whose job record is on again, off again: "we look in the file at their job record and see the same story over and over again—a job one week, then he quits it or gets fired and so on, and on. . . . He gets tired of this after awhile and we call him in on it."[13] When responding to a probation officer's request as to how well the ward in question was progressing on parole in light of a drug use conviction, the agent appeared to interpret the ward's job history as indicative of some kind of "progressive" failure.

Parole Status as Aggravation. The more general baseline consensus regarding sentencing, expressed explicitly in *California Rules of Court* (1977), is that a parole status itself is largely a liability. Rule 414, which stipulates criteria affecting probation, particularly Part d, Section 2, reads: "Prior performance on probation or parole and present probation *or* parole status" (p. 16). Rule 421 states that one circumstance that can be considered an *aggravation*, and in theory used to increase a prison term, is whether "The defendant was *on* probation or parole when he committed the crime" or whether "prior performance on probation or parole was *un*satisfactory." The only circumstance under which parole can be a mitigating factor is if "prior performance on probation or parole was *good*" (Rule 423, p. 19; emphases supplied).

Although this researcher has not ascertained the extent to which these rules have been officially invoked, their general message is clear: parole can more often be a significant liability at the point of sentencing than an asset. The implicit consensus of parole as an aggravation should be viewed within the context of overlapping parole and probation supervision and the cooperative relationship between the two agencies.

Detention, Case Processing, and Time to Dispositions

As noted earlier, the use of parole holds, making bail impossible, may indirectly structure the dynamics of the plea bargaining process. Only an accusation of wrongdoing is required; the bail offered to noncapital defendants, which involve "free" citizens, is specifically not extended to parolees. Other researchers have discussed the detriment an inability to make bail can have on dispositions (Thomas, 1976). One agent described his own case:

> Both the defense attorney and prosecutor know the advantage
> of having [the parolee] in jail for the prosecutor and we really
> catch it from the defense attorney. The guy can't be on the
> outside to prepare his case and he's more likely to plead guilty
> or cop the plea and accept credit for time served plus time on
> the copped plea. But it's not necessary to cop the plea since the
> guy's already in with no chance of getting out. So everyone waits
> until someone gets fed up or tired. Often it's the ward.[14]

Of course there are few materials in the present study on parole holds. In one of the few cases where documentation of a parole hold was available, a ward charged with assault to commit murder and robbery complained of his inadequate representation prior to a preliminary hearing and felt it should not begin. He had been interviewed only once while in jail. He had expected another, as his public defender had told him, but his attorney said it wasn't necessary and that the preliminary hearing should proceed. The parolee voiced further objections:

> Parolee: Also, the seriousness of this case and the fact that both
> the public defender and the officer involved in the crime of which
> I am accused are both employed by the same. . . .
> Court: That's, that's one of the most ill-founded objections. The
> public defender's office fights very hard and very diligently. And
> the fact that they're paid by the public—by the way, and so is the
> Court and so is the District Attorney, that one—I know it makes
> the rounds of the jails—does not appeal to me at all, doesn't prevent any one of us from doing our best in our job.[15]

The same parolee purportedly "blew up" in superior court over the issue of the quality of his legal representation and the judge requested psychiatric evaluations of him. The two evaluations, conducted at the jail, are revealing, if for no other reason than that both attempt to argue for his lack of "reason" for wanting a change of counsel but state that in other respects he is "sane." They first argued that the parolee's request for a court-appointed attorney rather than a public defender was "unyielding to reason." In this opinion the individual was a "youth who, under the stress of waiting for sentencing and facing the possibility of long-term incarceration, [was] hypercritical not only of the public defender but various phases of the process involved in his incarceration." The other evaluation was that "This highly impulsive young male is well institutionalized, manipulative and a 'latrine lawyer.' He quotes 'legalise' and cannot understand why his lawyer doesn't spend more time with him and attempts to be his own advocate." Yet oddly enough, even the judge recognized that the public defender had missed a scheduled appointment with his client.[16]

After his conviction and sentence to the C.Y.A. following a jury trial, the parolee persisted in his plea of innocence and wrote a lengthy letter to the director, but to no avail. The director eventually responded that the ward could appeal the decision if he so desired.

This case is an example of the restriction and narrowing of alternatives available to the detained, which may be inevitable when widely held assumptions that defendants will flee the jurisdiction and that parolees in particular pose a threat to themselves or others. But what is the evidence for the likelihood that those incarcerated would have been so disposed? As Robinson (1972) asks, "[W]ould every parolee fail to appear at trial if he were not detained by a parole hold?" Although the present data may not be complete, they indicate that only four of the discharges and four of the parolees failed to appear in court the entire follow-up period. In addition, two parolees and one discharged individual were charged with contempt of court and one discharge with failure to obey a court order. In any case, whatever the level of parolee detention, these data suggest that the discharges did not attempt to avoid appearance in court any more than did the parolees.

It is therefore unlikely that flight from prosecution can explain why the length of time taken to process parolee cases from the time of arrest to disposition was shorter than discharge cases. For all charges during the follow-up, as shown in Tables 6-5 and 6-6, the discharge offenses took an average of 4.9 months for disposition, the parolees 4.0. The difference is greatest for personal crimes, where the average time to disposition was 6.4 for the discharges and only 4.3 months for the parolees. Time to dispositions for property offenses is quite similar between the two groups but the discharges took longer to all other offenses, including drug and alcohol offenses, than the parolees (4.5 and 3.2 months, respectively). True, there is a considerable amount of missing data here, specifically, 47 percent of the charges for both groups, due in no small

Table 6-5. Months to Disposition by Nature of Offense: Parolees

Months to disposition	Total No.	Total %	Parolees Personal No.	Parolees Personal %	Property No.	Property %	All other No.	All other %
No information	246	46.9	39	37.1	123	55.6	84	42.2
30 days or less	91	17.3	21	20.0	17	7.7	53	26.6
2 months	36	6.9	7	6.7	17	7.7	12	6.0
3 months	33	6.3	6	5.7	13	5.9	14	7.0
4 months	22	4.2	5	4.8	8	3.6	9	4.5
5 months	15	2.9	5	4.8	4	1.8	6	3.0
6 months	18	3.4	6	5.7	6	2.7	6	3.0
7 months	16	3.0	4	3.8	7	3.2	5	2.5
8 or more months	48	9.1	12	11.4	26	11.8	10	5.0
Total	525	100.0	105	100.0	221	100.0	199	100.0
Average	4.0		4.3		5.3		3.2	

Note: Percentages may not add to 100.0 due to errors in rounding.

Table 6-6. Months to Disposition by Nature of Offense: Discharges

Months to disposition	Total		Discharges Personal		Property		All other	
	No.	%	No.	%	No.	%	No.	%
No information	121	46.7	15	33.3	54	56.8	52	43.7
30 days or less	38	14.7	11	24.4	7	7.4	20	16.8
2 months	18	6.9	5	11.1	2	2.1	11	9.2
3 months	20	7.7	5	11.1	6	6.3	9	7.6
4 months	13	5.0	0	—	6	6.3	7	5.9
5 months	10	3.9	3	6.7	4	4.2	3	2.5
6 months	7	2.7	2	4.4	3	3.2	2	1.7
7 months	7	2.7	1	2.2	3	3.2	3	2.5
8 or more months	25	9.6	3	6.7	10	10.5	12	10.1
Total	259	100.0	45	100.0	95	100.0	119	100.0
Average	4.9		6.4		5.5		4.5	

Note: Percentages may not add to 100.0 due to errors in rounding.

part to the expense of obtaining this information. Assuming, however, that the reasons for the lack of data are similar, the findings suggest that personal crimes of the parolees were processed much more quickly than those of the discharges.

It may be, then, that parole agents facilitated the work of probation officers by providing the latter with information otherwise unavailable to them. Parole holds, at whatever level they were used, may have sped up the plea bargaining and much less-used trial process. The difference in time to dispositions could also have been due to the differential nature of the evidence required for disposition of the two groups' charges. It also could be that the parolees were charged with offenses that were more easily resolvable than discharge offenses.

CHAPTER SUMMARY

The data of the present study do not support the deterrence argument that parole reduces crime. They suggest instead that parole may merely alter its form in such a way as to make the crime more serious and secondary in nature. It appears, then, that the deterrence argument does not apply to individuals in this study who have been convicted and stigmatized. This possibility has been recognized by deterrence theorists.

The data also suggest that a parole status may have consequences at the point of sentencing—in other words, that it may play a role in defining the nature and extent of parolee failure. Although the supervisory status of parole alone does not appear to affect the timing or length of probation, investigation of these questions reveals a significant amount of overlapping supervision between probation and parole, the consequences of which remain uncertain. Even where dual jurisdiction does not exist the formal and informal practice of probation and parole agent cooperation may result in agent-instigated court dispositions, which contradict the board policy that ultimate say in C.Y.A. disposition is theirs. Since the latter policy is conditioned by what occurs in court in the bulk of cases,[17] an exception being drug offenses, parole agent participation in both board and court dispositions may be a significant source of influence in case dispositions.

These observations suggest official categorizations have consequences, and that the activities of officials are relevant in producing spurious recidivism at the level of disposition. We might say, tentatively, that parole generates more serious crime and then amplifies the consequences associated with conviction among individuals who may be least deterrable, due in part to their parole status.

NOTES

1. See Waldo and Chiricos (1972), who found that marijuana offenses were more readily deterred the greater the perceived certainty of punishment. Silberman (1976) was unable to replicate the finding for another student population.

2. I have argued that the growth of unmarried cohabitation is in part a result of attenuated familial controls over courtship. Discovery of the relationship by parents often "forced" a definition of the relationship, which resulted in marriage (Jackson, 1983).

3. The parolees in the present study do not appear to differ greatly from the entire C.Y.A. parole population in percentage charged with homicide and in sentences to adult prison. Of the 5,765 parolees violated during 1976, 1.1 percent were for homicide. In the present study 3 percent of all (198) parolees were charged with homicide. The figures may not be comparable because it is unclear what the implications are of following a select cohort through time for 26 months, as has been done here, and comparing their outcomes with all individuals on parole during the course of a year. Figures on the percentage sentenced to adult prison can be found in Appendix 1. Interestingly, the percentage sentenced to adult prison in the total C.Y.A. population shown in Appendix 1 is greatest among those with between 7 and 18 months prior parole, as found in the present data. These data are not shown here.

4. Taken from court transcripts.

5. Presentence investigation made in early 1978.

6. Taken from court transcripts in Alameda Superior Court, late 1976.

7. This is one of the primary differences between McCleary's (1978) study and the present one. The exercise of influence in the justice system here is more covert.

8. Interview notes taken in July 1979.

9. Interview notes taken in July 1979.

10. Interview notes taken in July 1979.

11. Interview notes taken in July 1979.

12. Telephone interview of June 1979.

13. Interview notes taken in July 1979.

14. Interview notes taken in July 1979.

15. Interview notes taken in July 1979.

16. Taken from court transcripts, May 1977.

17. The outcomes of C.Y.A. board actions were closely defined by court actions in this study. Violations for "technicals" usually, but not always, exchanged C.Y.A. institution time for jail time. The two exceptions, one drug-related, prove the general rule. The modal disposition for violation actions in the C.Y.A. was to continue on parole; court-ordered commitments to C.D.C. resulted in dishonorable discharges to adult prison; mixed sentences to jail and probation resulted in general discharges or continuance, the former when custody time was exhausted by the length of time to be spent in jail or on probation.

7
Summary and Conclusions

SUMMARY

This study proposes that parole reveals a paradox of social control; that is, that it does not reduce crime and may even exacerbate the very problem it seeks to control. Past research showing positive effects of parole supervision were found to be biased on a priori grounds, plagued with problems of comparability of outcome measures, or in some cases riddled with unwarranted assumptions about the nature of parole supervision—assumptions that make it impossible to test its effects. Studies that control for selection of parolees find either no effects or small effects of supervision (Waller, 1974).

However, no previous research examined the effects of random discharge from parole supervision. With this in mind the present study compared the subsequent record of arrests, convictions, nature of charges and sentences, and time in custody of two randomly assigned groups: one retained on parole and the other completely discharged from California Youth Authority jurisdiction.

The study results contradict earlier findings for adults based on quasi-experimental designs, which show that parole postpones recidivism, that low-risk offenders are most likely to benefit from parole (Sacks and Logan, 1979), and that parole reduces the likelihood of arrest (Lerner, 1977). The arrest and conviction outcome data are generally consistent with past research using randomized designs to test the effects of minimal supervision (Star, 1979; Hudson, 1972) and in line with studies of the effects of early discharge from parole (Jaman, Bennett, and Berecochea, 1974; Bennett and Ziegler, 1975), which suggest that long-term retention on parole may not be worth all the costs.

Twenty-six months after the starting date of March 1, 1976, the parolees were found to have been convicted of significantly more serious charges. The difference in severity of charges was primarily due to the differing offenses the two groups were charged with: the parolees were more likely to be charged with violent personal crimes of homicide and rape and property offenses while the discharges were far more likely to be charged with drug- and alcohol-related offenses. Nonetheless, the overall percentage arrested and convicted did not differ between the two groups. Nor were there any differences in time to offenses, number of arrests, quarterly percentage in custody, percentage arrested while correcting for the number at risk in the community, and overall time spent in custody in jail, C.Y.A., and adult prison combined.

Findings relating to outcome by prior time spent on parole are revealing: parolees who had spent somewhat longer prior time on parole at the starting time of the study performed worse than the discharges. Although there were some small differences favoring the parolees among those with six or fewer months prior parole, the evidence is stronger for the conclusion that long-term retention on parole supervision may have deleterious consequences.

Previous research using the Interpersonal Maturity Level classification in the Community Treatment Project (Palmer, 1974) found that I-Level was significantly related to more favorable outcomes among individuals released to the community rather than being held in institutions. The present study has compared the outcomes between the parolees and discharges by major I-Level classifications (that is, I-3's and I-4's) and found no difference in outcome. These findings suggest the I-Level classification may not be a useful means for selecting individuals for discharge from parole and may shed some light on interpreting the relationship between caseload size, I-Level and outcome some find puzzling (Lipton, Martinson, and Wilks, 1975).

The present study also suggests that the influence of parole is specific to certain categories of parolees. Precisely how and why this occurs is worthy of future research. Prior work has shown that certain offenders are more likely than others to show negative effects from "labeling." Studies by Jensen (1972) and Ageton and Elliot (1974) suggest that labeling influences on self-concept or delinquent orientations, respectively, are found among whites more than blacks, which is supported in part here for the likelihood of conviction. And Thornberry (1971) also found that less serious offenders and whites were more likely to show measurable labeling effects after stigmatization, in the form of more serious offenses. Consistent with these findings, offenders in the present study with less serious prior records had less severe subsequent offenses and were less likely to have spent time in custody.

The differential reaction to parolee recidivism found in previous studies (Star, 1979; Hudson, 1972), due largely to the differential processing of cases under minimal or summary parole, is also found in this study. Discharges with less severe charges were more likely to receive probation. Parolee charges were disposed of more quickly than those of the discharges, particularly nonproperty-related offenses.

Parolee charges related to crimes against the person were more likely to result in state prison sentences than those of the discharges. Part of this differential in sentences can be attributed to the seriousness of offenses of the parolees (viz., homicide and to a lesser extent rape). It is suggested that the imposition of active social control may modify the behavior of parolees by providing alternative structural contexts within which drift toward criminal activity can occur. This process may occur in conjunction with, or have the effect of, preventing maturational reform. In the present situation, due to the visible nature of drug- and alcohol-related crimes and therefore the possibility of their detection by agents, those retained on parole were much less likely to be charged with this category of offense. Instead they were charged with violent personal crimes and property crimes. In this regard, deterrence theory predictions fail for this sample of youthful offenders. The data fail to support the general argument that parole will reduce or prevent all kinds of crimes through the threat of imprisonment. It may be that this is a result of implied assumptions of the theory, which suggest that attempts at deterrence can either *reduce* crime or have *no* effects, but rarely *alter the form or nature* of illegal acts. In the present case it appears that the behavior coming to the attention of officials was more serious and secondary in nature.

Sentences to adult prison for more serious parolee charges were due at least in part to influences of a parole status in choice-making contexts at the individual level. Yet even for personal offenses other than homicide and rape the likelihood of sentence to adult prison was greater for parolees. Both organizational and demographic factors may have contributed to this pattern: the age of the parolees convicted of these offenses, the length of time remaining in their sentences—which was shorter than the discharges charged with similar offenses—and the fact that a parole status is conceived of as a circumstance in aggravation at the level of sentencing.

The lesser time taken to clear parolee arrests suggested that organizational factors may have speeded up their processing. For example, it may be that the use of parole holds facilitated the plea bargaining process. However, definite conclusions are difficult because we have no data on where and how often they were used, and the parolees were arrested for more serious charges—crimes that may be more quickly resolved. It may be that the mere fact of parole officer input through the probation officer, a long-standing informal practice of cooperation exercised by the C.Y.A., speeded up the justice process by saving the probation officer work. Given the apparent tendency of probation officers to follow the recommendations of parole officers, this explanation for the difference in processing time is more credible. There are, however, no "hard" data on the extent to which probation officers follow recommendations of parole officers.

One intended or unintended effect of such informal cooperation may have been more punitive treatment of the parolees. To what extent parole officers "turned their backs" on the somewhat older, black parolees committed for personal and property crimes, who figured prominently in sentences to prison, is an open question. In many respects these were "end of the line" cases: there was little time for another C.Y.A. incarceration-parole loop—what one parole officer called "burning them out." For others age was prohibitive of a new commitment. Common to all was a formal and perhaps more importantly informal agreement to stay out of trouble, which was broken. The choice of agent recommendations may therefore have been a foregone conclusion.

This situation, one confronting the older youthful offender faced with a parole staff geared toward younger, "unsophisticated" delinquents of days past in the C.Y.A. captures the plight of youthful offenders today and defines this juncture as a turning point in their future lives.

Taken together, these findings offer tentative support for Studt's (1967) thesis. The existence of more serious crimes among the parolees lends credence to the idea that parolees "who are exposed to an unrelieved experience of high risk develop some sort of defensive adaptations [which] may assume the behavioral guise of either low commitment or habitual flirting with danger" (1967, pp. 3-4). Because of the significantly greater seriousness of the parolee offenses and differential reaction based upon a parole status, the greater likelihood of a parolee sentence to adult prison rather than the C.Y.A. defines a parole status as a mechanism of status placement to adult prison for youthful offenders.

THE ILLUSION OF CONTROL
AND SOME UNINTENDED CONSEQUENCES

There are many reasons why one would not expect the mere fact of parole supervision to reduce crime in the community. In Chapter 4, for instance, it was pointed out that the parole process consists of a reactive enterprise directed toward resolving parolee crime that has already occurred. Like probation officers, parole officers often describe supervision as the business of "putting out fires." Yet there are other reasons. Agents, for example, do not have the technology to prevent crime (Studt, 1973). Studt's observation that agents are incapable of making judgments about possible future crimes is a devastating criticism of the assumption that agents can prevent crime through use of detention.

Moreover, indirect means taken to prevent or reduce crime through counseling are seriously impeded by the fact that parole supervision is involuntary. What little interaction occurs between parolees and agents tends to be bland and diffuse and superficially friendly due to the potential jeopardy inherent in it for the parolee. The numerous, conflicting, and vague parole rules create a constant potential for return to prison. And as Parker (1975, p. 36) argues: "most free citizens would find it difficult to avoid violations of parole regulations if all were rigorously enforced."

While parole supervision is therefore pervasive in potential effects on the parolee's liberty and livelihood, it is also narrow in scope. The argument that the officer can ameliorate the problems of criminogenic influences of peers, poverty, broken homes, and discrimination and overcome class and cultural differences existing between him and his charges with the limited services and resources at his or her disposal can only be regarded as utopian. Agents can not, of course, follow their parolees 24 hours a day. As with the probation officer (Emerson, 1969, p. 221), in general "it is the *threat* of incarceration that provides the [parole] officer with his main weapon for affecting the behavior of his [parolees]" (emphasis in original).

Parolee perceptions of parole supervision challenge the assumption that supervision deters them from committing crimes. For example, career criminal researchers who queried habitual offenders as to whether a parole officer's supervision affected their involvement in crime found little evidence to support the argument (Petersilia, Greenwood, and Lavin, 1977, p. 51). The researchers did find that an officer's supervision did affect a parolee's involvement in crime to a slightly greater extent during a juvenile period of criminal activity than during an adult period. Yet during both periods of criminal activity between 10.5 percent and 11.5 percent of the felons interviewed felt that parole supervision actually *encouraged* their involvement in crime. Nonetheless, by far the most common response to the question was that parole officers have no effect on involvement in crime.

Two-thirds of the parolees in Waller's (1974) study felt there was much more freedom on parole than they had expected. Morris and Beverly (1975) p. 130) also found that the modal perception of probation officers by parolees was "very helpful but free and easy." A small but significant percentage of the parolees in the latter study also felt they were "thought of as a criminal" due to their parole status and that people would expect they would break rules *because* they were parolees. Taken in conjunction with the findings of Petersilia, Greenwood, and Lavin, the latter findings suggest the assumed deterrent function of parole supervision is negligible except for drug offenses and that this manifest aim of supervision may well foster perceptions among parolees that they will, indeed, get into "trouble."

These considerations suggest that parole supervision implicitly serves purposes other than the reduction of crime. Parole may serve a symbolic function, one which in a Durkheimian vein reinforces various beliefs or myths. In discussing some of the reasons why parole should exist, for example, Waller (1972, p. 133) identified "the need to placate public opinion with the claim that justice is being done and protection [is] being given, even though criminals are being set free." Of course the other reasons why parole exists can be easily identified: overcrowding in prisons, the monies required to build new prisons, the precarious situation of prisoners exiting institutions, and the needs of the parole function to "stay in business" are all a justification of the system.

But the importance of parole in providing an illusion of control, thereby supporting myths, should not be ignored any more than the myths of police work (Manning, 1977, pp. 324-332). The myth at work can be found in the writings of British thinkers attempting to grapple with emergent problems of their newly developed parole release and supervision procedures. They find that "At present the newspapers and the public show a concern for crimes committed by parolees that is ridiculously at variance with their lack of interest in crimes committed by ex-prisoners who are released without supervision" (West, 1972, p. 24, quoted in Bottomley, 1973, p. 211). One might suggest that this problem is inherent in situations where public agencies purport to achieve goals that cannot be met. The core issue, in any case, is the legitimacy of the institution.[1]

The threat to the legitimacy of parole raised by parolee crime and exposure of the underlying myths by public recognition of the illusion of control are suggested in *People v. Denne* (141 California Appellate 2d 499), where it is written:

> [T]he public is entitled to a maximum protection in the
> administration of the parole system. . . . Many a vicious crime
> is committed by a parolee, *shocking the faith of the public* in
> the efficacy and desirability of parole (emphasis supplied; taken
> from Gottesman and Hecker, 1963, p. 703).

Note that even though the concern here is with the protection afforded the public, it is also revealing to see that flagrant instances of its ineffectiveness shock the "faith of the public." Manning (1977, p. 326) suggests a reason for this in stating that, "A myth alleviates societal crises by providing a verbal explanation for causes, meanings, and consequences of events that might otherwise be considered inexplicable." Thus a parolee in "trouble" whose alleged or documented actions attract public attention violates the assumption that an agency responsible for the behavior of its charges should not allow criminal behavior to occur.

The argument of corrections agencies that they can, in fact, effectively prevent, reduce, or control crime through parole supervision has unanticipated consequences for both parolees and the organization, which is the important point here. For example, the C.Y.A. has been faced with victims' lawsuits against corrections authorities for parolee crimes. At present it appears the state can be held financially liable "if there is negligence in parole supervision which is the proximate cause of an inquiry." One victim received a settlement of $225,000 for injuries; a recent claim seeking a million dollars in damages alleges there was a "failure to rehabilitate" (California Department of the Youth Authority, *Annual Plan*, 1978, p. 35).

The parolee, in turn, suffers from the illusion because his fate within the system can and does become tied to the reactions of public groups, the media, and others; the stigma of parole defines such an individual as "dangerous." This is particularly true among adult parolees committed to prison for person crimes. Neithercutt (1972, p. 89) found, for example, that *"person offenders are being returned to prison on a different set of criteria than are property offenders*, a set of criteria which holds the former to a much more rigid (and arbitrary) standard of conduct" (emphasis in original). Aside from perceived and real harm to victims, the subsequent reaction to alleged or actual parolee crime is at once both a visible, embarrassing reminder of correctional failure and an attempt to reinstate the legitimacy of parole. The price of such a system of punishment, in Mead's (1928, p. 601) formulation, is a failure to repress crime and the preservation of a "criminal class."

Finally, the legitimization of the ideology that parole supervision can control crime—recently under strong attack—has undoubtedly prevented systematic study to determine the effects, intended or unintended, of parole supervision. Studies by social scientists that call into question the underlying legitimacy of social programs ipso facto weaken or destroy the myths on which they rest. As Boulding (1966, p. 97) has noted, albeit awkwardly:

> One of the sources of legitimacy in any society is that the legitimate is simply not called into question. The moment an ancient legitimacy is called into question it is often very deeply threatened, simply because where legitimacy depends on something not being questioned, the very asking of a question threatens it in a way that cannot be answered with any answer. The only answer to asking the question is, don't ask the question; and this is one thing that in a social-science culture is illegitimate.

The informal history of the present project, found in Appendix 3 bears out this argument—that attempts to ascertain the effects of parole itself were not widely held as legitimate.

REORIENTATION OF CORRECTIONS

The major policy implication is that some parolees can be randomly discharged from parole without increased risk to the public. The study thus helps to pave the way for a much larger study, which could include direct discharge from institutions for selected offenders. Yet even the National Advisory Commission on Criminal Justice Standards and Goals (1973) wrote some time before the recent controversy over parole supervision that

> A piece of research evidence which has been validated repeatedly
> . . . is that a significant number of parolees can do very well with

little official supervision. . . . Most of these parolees probably should
be released from any form of supervision at all. Outright discharge
from the institution would be an appropriate disposition and should
be used much more frequently than it is. . . .

These considerations help explain why parole is currently undergoing a
major reassessment in this country. Even more impressive than the voluminous
criticism of the institution are the concrete actions taken by a number of states
in transferring the powers to set sentences to the courts or sentencing review
boards. Although most of these changes have (by definition) been imposed on
the parole release decision by legislation, the net effect in most cases has been
to diminish the length of community control over parolees through time restrictions on jurisdiction over prisoners. Only one state, Maine, has completely
abolished both parole release and community supervision.

Much research needs to be carried out on the effects of this new legislation,
especially as it concerns revamping the parole supervision component of parole.
Removing or delimiting the threat of revocation undercuts the traditional justification of community supervision. It is therefore not surprising that community
supervision is currently undergoing a reassessment of goals and means.

At present a number of alternative means of release are being considered.
One is contract parole, not discussed further here. A second is retention of traditional parole supervision. Another is a voluntary services approach wherein
services are rendered at parolee request. The final one is total and complete
discharge from any form of supervision whatsoever. When determinate sentencing is taken to its conclusion—at least in theory—complete discharge from any
form of supervision is one alternative given the current assumptions underlying
community supervision.

The present study adds to our knowledge about the effects of parole supervision in an important way. Viewed in light of research by Hudson (1972) and
Star (1979) on the efficacy of minimal supervision and of summary parole—akin
to voluntary services—the present findings that there are no beneficial effects of
traditional parole under an indefinite sentencing system suggest that none of the
alternatives is likely to diminish recidivism. In fact, the traditional alternative
of release of prisoners under supervision may create unintended costs beyond
dollars and cents through creating and maintaining a correctional system that
reinforces the very crime it seeks to control. Given this, the systematic reassessment of goals and means of community supervision and their change is an
eminent possibility.

NOTE

1. The parolee in trouble questions what one author refers to as the "functional legitimacy" of, in this case, parole (Yankelovich, 1974, pp. 528-530; cf. Herz, 1978). Functional legitimacy refers to the extent to which the public feels that governmental policies or practices are effective in providing basic services necessary for living: fire protection, garbage disposal, driveable roads, as well as protection from crime of "known" criminals.

Appendix 1
Exclusions from Random Assignment

The original study design called for a more extended and comprehensive study of the individuals, and the exclusions, in part, reflect this goal. Table A1-1 shows the number and percent of exclusions.

Table A1-1. Exclusions from Random Assignment

	No.	%
Total wards on parole lists	725	100.0%
Exclusions from random assignment	411	56.7
Reasons for exclusion	411	100.0
1. On full board status	103	25.1
2. On special service status	23	5.6
3. On violation status	134	32.6
4. End jurisdiction by 7/1/76	73	17.8
5. Transfer pending	36	8.8
6. Residence outside area	23	5.6
7. Out-of-state case	15	3.6
8. No file available		1.2
Total eligible wards	314	43.3

Appendix 2
Sample Representatives

This section shows how the study cases compare in background characteristics and demographic information with the remainder of the parolees on parole
as of December 31, 1975, the period closest to the random assignment for which
data are available.

REPRESENTATIVENESS OF SAMPLE

Ideally a comparison of the study groups to the remaining parolees in the
state would examine data current as of the end of January 1976, the point at
which the parole lists were current. Unfortunately, comparison data are not
available for January 1976, but are for all parole cases as of December 1975.
It appears reasonable to assume that the data are a close but not perfect approximation of that existing in January 1976. As it turned out, 706 of the 725 cases
on the parole lists current as of January 1976, in the study area were on parole
in the same location in December 1975.

Three comparisons are made below: 1. between the area chosen for study
and the remainder of the state; 2. between the cases excluded from and included
in the study; and 3. between the study groups and the remainder of the state.
In all comparisons out-of-state cases have been excluded.

Study Area and December 1975 Parolees

A total of 689 parolees were located in the three parole unit locations in
December 1975. And in the remainder of the state there were 6,874 individuals
on parole. Thus the study area comprised 9.1 percent of the C.Y.A.'s youthful
offender parole population. How typical are the study area parolees of the
remainder of the state?

Table A2-1 shows the number and percent of various categories of parolees
by selected demographic and background characteristics. Column one is the
total parole population minus the study groups, column two is the total parole
population minus those individuals in the study area (n = 689); column three
includes individuals in the study area who were excluded from random assignment and who were on parole in the study area as of December 1975; column
four includes the individuals randomly assigned to one of the experimental conditions; and column five is the exclusions and study groups combined. Column
five does not add up to 689 because of the small number of cases added to the
December 1975 parole lists in January 1976.

Table A2-1. Background Characteristics of Total Agency Population, Study Area Exclusions, and Study Groups

Characteristics	(1) Total 12/31/75 Parolees No.	%	(2) 12/31/75 Parolees Less Exclusions No.	%	(3) Exclusions No.	%	(4) Study Groups No.	%	(5) Exclusions and Study Groups No.	%
Total	7,284	100.0	6,874	100.0	410	100.0	296	100.0	706	100.0
Sex										
Male	6,601	90.6	6,238	90.7	363	88.5	275	92.9	638	90.4
Female	683	9.4	636	9.2	47	11.5	21	7.1	68	9.6
Race										
White	3,373	46.3	3,225	46.9	148	36.1	103	34.8	251	35.5
Black	2,315	31.8	2,092	30.4	223	54.4	165	55.7	388	55.0
All other	1,596	21.9	1,557	22.6	39	9.5	28	9.4	67	9.5
Prior record										
None	301	4.1	284	4.1	17	4.1	15	5.1	32	4.5
Contact only	3,136	43.1	2,963	43.1	173	42.2	107	36.1	280	39.7
One commitment	2,297	31.5	2,162	31.4	135	32.9	97	32.8	232	32.9
2+ commitments	1,550	21.3	1,465	21.3	85	20.7	77	26.0	162	22.9
Court										
Juvenile	3,624	49.8	3,400	49.5	224	54.6	137	46.3	361	51.1
Adult	3,660	50.2	3,474	50.5	186	45.4	159	53.7	345	48.9
Base expectancy score										
Females (none)	683	9.4	636	9.2	47	11.5	21	7.1	68	12.6
1 (low)	1,557	21.4	1,493	21.7	64	15.6	78	26.4	142	20.1
2	1,912	26.2	1,804	26.2	108	26.3	102	34.5	210	29.7
3	1,530	21.0	1,448	21.1	82	20.0	36	12.2	118	16.7
4	1,483	20.4	1,387	20.2	96	23.4	33	11.1	129	18.3
5 (high)	119	1.6	106	1.5	13	3.2	26	8.8	39	5.5

Admission status										
1st commitment	5,104	70.1	4,846	70.5	258	62.9	215	72.6	473	67.0
Parole violator	1,149	15.8	1,072	15.6	77	18.8	43	14.5	120	17.0
Recommitment	1,031	14.2	956	13.9	75	18.3	38	12.8	113	16.0
Full Board status										
Never on	5,742	78.8	5,455	79.4	287	70.0	292	98.6	579	82.0
On 1st time	1,464	20.1	1,344	19.6	120	29.3	0	0.0	120	17.0
Off was on	78	1.1	75	1.1	3	0.7	4	1.4	7	0.9
Special Service										
Never on	5,219	71.7	4,925	71.6	294	71.7	288	97.3	582	82.4
On 1st time	1,727	23.7	1,624	23.6	103	25.1	0	0.0	103	14.6
Off was on	200	2.7	196	2.8	4	1.0	8	2.7	12	1.7
On was on	138	1.9	129	1.9	9	2.2	0	0.0	9	1.3
Parole violations										
None	6,506	89.3	6,139	89.3	367	89.5	239	80.7	606	85.8
One	543	7.5	510	7.4	33	8.0	44	14.9	77	10.9
Two or more	235	3.2	225	3.3	10	2.4	13	4.4	23	3.2
Recommitments										
None	6,709	92.1	6,332	92.1	377	92.0	250	84.5	627	88.8
One	489	6.7	461	6.7	28	6.8	43	14.5	71	10.0
Two or more	86	1.2	81	1.2	5	1.2	3	1.0	8	1.1
Parole returns										
None	5,104	70.1	4,846	70.5	258	62.9	215	72.6	473	67.0
One	1,376	18.9	1,282	18.6	94	22.9	50	16.9	144	20.4
Two or more	804	11.0	746	10.8	58	14.1	31	10.5	89	12.6

Characteristics	No.	%	No.	%	No.	%	No.	%	No.	%
Prior escapes										
None	5,820	79.9	5,502	80.0	318	77.6	232	78.4	550	77.9
One	941	12.9	885	12.9	56	13.7	37	12.5	93	13.2
Two or more	502	6.9	468	6.8	34	8.3	21	7.1	55	7.8
Unknown	21	0.3	19	0.3	2	0.5	6	2.0	8	1.1
Parole location										
Richmond	145	2.0	0	–	145	35.4	82	27.7	227	32.1
Hayward	127	1.7	0	–	127	31.0	113	38.3	240	34.0
Oakland	138	1.9	0	–	138	33.7	101	34.2	239	33.8
All other	6,874	94.4	6,874	100.0	0	–	0	–	0	–
Commitment offense										
Person	2,280	31.3	2,152	31.3	128	31.2	74	25.0	202	28.6
Property	2,807	38.5	2,644	38.5	163	39.8	154	52.0	317	44.9
Drug and Alcohol	691	9.5	665	9.7	26	6.3	19	6.4	45	6.4
Other	1,506	20.7	1,413	20.6	93	22.7	49	16.6	142	20.1
Commitment offense by % violation at 24 months on										
Welfare and Institution (53.5%)	864	11.9	806	11.7	58	14.1	30	10.1	88	12.5
Other (50.5%)	406	5.6	388	5.6	18	4.4	17	5.7	35	5.0
Theft (49.9%)	1,302	17.9	1,222	17.8	80	19.5	68	23.0	148	21.0
Burglary (46.5%)	1,505	20.7	1,422	20.7	83	20.2	86	29.0	169	23.9
Sex (45.3%)	236	3.2	219	3.2	17	4.1	2	0.7	19	2.7
Assault (40.7%)	715	9.8	681	9.9	34	8.3	17	5.7	51	7.2
Robbery (40.5%)	1,402	19.2	1,317	19.2	85	20.7	57	19.2	142	20.1
Drug/Narcotics (30%)	691	9.5	665	9.7	26	6.3	19	6.4	45	6.4
Homicide (25.0%)	163	2.2	154	2.2	9	2.2	0	–	9	1.3

Prior months on parole 3/1/76									
	1,563	21.5	1,498	21.8	65	15.9	88	29.7	153	21.7
1-6	1,563	21.5	1,498	21.8	65	15.9	88	29.7	153	21.7
7-12	1,725	23.7	1,625	23.6	100	24.4	65	22.0	165	23.4
13-18	1,254	17.2	1,176	17.1	78	19.0	51	17.2	129	18.3
19-24	907	12.5	863	12.6	44	10.7	25	8.4	69	9.8
25-30	593	8.1	563	8.2	30	7.3	16	5.4	46	6.5
31-36	413	5.7	381	5.5	32	7.8	21	7.1	53	7.5
37-42	314	4.3	294	4.3	20	4.9	10	3.4	30	4.2
43 and over	515	7.1	474	6.9	41	10.0	20	6.8	61	8.6
Median	14.0		13.9		14.9		11.8		12.5	
Age as of 3/1/76										
17 and under	406	5.6	386	5.6	20	4.9	15	5.1	35	5.0
18	613	8.4	588	8.6	25	6.1	36	12.2	61	8.6
19	1,038	14.3	981	14.3	57	13.9	52	17.6	109	15.4
20	1,365	18.7	1,271	18.5	94	22.9	65	22.0	159	22.5
21	1,429	19.6	1,340	19.5	89	21.7	45	15.2	134	19.0
22	1,033	14.2	982	14.3	51	12.4	52	17.6	103	14.6
23	827	11.4	774	11.2	53	12.9	21	7.1	74	10.5
24-25	573	7.9	552	8.0	21	5.1	10	3.4	31	4.4
Median	20.0		20.0		20.0		19.3		19.4	
Months from latest admission to parole										
5 and under	992	13.6	952	13.8	40	9.9	40	13.5	80	11.3
6-8	1,663	22.8	1,562	22.7	101	24.6	91	30.7	192	27.2
9-12	1,914	26.3	1,813	26.4	101	24.6	100	33.8	201	28.5
13-15	1,141	15.7	1,083	15.8	58	14.1	38	12.8	96	13.6
16 and over	1,574	21.6	1,464	21.3	110	26.8	27	9.1	137	19.4
Median	10.65		10.63		11.35		9.26		8.7	

Characteristics	No.	%	No.	%	No.	%	No.	%	No.	%
Prior months under jurisdiction at 3/1/76										
12 and under	373	5.1	360	5.2	13	3.2	25	8.4	38	5.4
13-18	776	10.6	749	10.9	27	6.6	48	16.2	75	10.6
19-24	1,020	14.0	971	14.1	49	12.0	47	15.9	96	13.6
25-30	899	12.3	854	12.4	45	11.0	33	11.1	78	11.0
31-36	879	12.1	829	12.0	50	12.2	31	10.5	81	11.5
37-42	705	9.7	672	9.8	33	8.0	20	6.8	53	7.5
43-48	577	7.9	541	7.9	36	8.8	19	6.4	55	7.8
49-54	434	6.0	407	5.9	27	6.6	16	5.4	43	6.1
55-60	370	5.1	344	5.0	26	6.3	18	6.1	44	6.2
61-66	279	3.8	260	3.8	19	4.6	9	3.0	28	4.0
67-72	244	3.3	223	3.2	21	5.1	11	3.7	32	4.5
73 and over	728	10.0	664	9.6	64	15.6	21	7.1	85	12.0
Median	34.8		34.6		39.5		29.2		31.1	
Sentence length										
1-3 years	1,145	15.7	1,091	15.9	54	13.2	15	5.1	69	9.8
4 years	1,883	25.9	1,794	26.1	89	21.7	51	17.2	140	19.8
5 years	1,653	22.7	1,556	22.6	97	23.7	81	27.4	178	25.2
6 years	1,360	18.7	1,286	18.7	74	18.0	75	25.3	149	21.1
7 years	572	7.9	530	7.7	42	10.2	36	12.2	78	11.0
8 or more years	671	9.2	617	9.0	54	13.2	38	12.8	92	13.0
Median (in months)	58.0		57.8		61.7		60.8		58.8	

[a]Excludes study group cases (n = 296) and out-of-state supervision.

122

Of interest here is the comparison between columns two and three, which indicate the general characteristics of individuals in the study area compared to the remainder of the state. There are no large differences in sex, prior record of delinquent contacts and commitments, base expectancy scores, Special Service status, parole violations, number of recommitments, prior escapes, commitment offense, median number of prior parole months for the most recent parole stay, median age, and median time in institutions prior to the most recent parole. There are some differences in race, which was expected: 55 percent of the study area parolees are black compared to 30 percent of the remainder of the state. There are also fewer Mexican-American and other ethnic groups among those in the study area. The area also has a higher percentage of juvenile court commitments, a slightly higher percentage of court recommitments for the most recent admission to the C.Y.A., Full Board cases, and parole returns. Parolees in the remainder of the state show a higher median number of months remaining in jurisdiction at the time of the study starting date, as well as a higher median number of months under jurisdiction than the study area parolees. Finally, the median length of time from first admission to jurisdiction termination is slightly higher for individuals in the study area.

Study Groups and Exclusions

The comparison between the cases eventually chosen for study and those excluded from the pool of eligibles (columns three and four) reveals the intended (and perhaps unintended) effects of the use of the various exclusionary criteria on the background characteristics of the study cases. How did the exclusionary criteria affect the composition of the study groups?

As one would expect, most of the Full Board and Special Service parole cases ended up in the exclusions (all such cases eventually did by the time of the study starting date). Most sex violators and all homicide cases were also excluded. Interestingly, there was a rise among the study cases in the percentage with a commitment offense of burglary and theft—individuals with a high likelihood of violating parole at 24 months. The percent of study group cases with a commitment offense involving property is 52 percent, and among the exclusions 40 percent. Study group cases are also likely to have two or more prior commitments to facilities other than the C.Y.A., to be adult court cases, to be a first commitment rather than a parole violator, to have spent less time on parole as of March 1, 1976, to have a greater median number of months remaining in jurisdiction, and to have spent less time under C.Y.A. jurisdiction.

Study Groups and Remaining Parolees in the State

There are no large differences between the study groups and remaining parolees in the state with respect to sex, court of commitment, admission status, number of parole returns, escapes, and age. There are moderate differences in time spent in institutions before the most recent parole and total amount of time spent under C.Y.A. jurisdiction as of March 1, 1976, with the study groups showing less time than the remaining parolees on these items. The remaining parolees had a higher median number of months left in jurisdiction as of March 1, 1976, slightly shorter overall sentence lengths than the study cases, and more median prior months on the most recent parole. There are, of course, large and expected differences in parole location, Full Board, and Special Service status cases. There is some fluctuation in base expectancy scores but the overall difference is not too great.

There are, however, fairly substantial differences in race, differences which reflect the character of the study area, as noted above. Of the parolees who were not in the study 46 percent were white, while only 35 percent of the study groups individuals were white. And 56 percent of the study group was black compared to only 32 percent of the remaining parolees in the state. The study groups also had a higher percentage of cases with two or more prior local commitments, and a greater number of cases with one or more parole violations and recommitments. Finally, the study groups also show a greater percentage of cases with commitment offenses of theft and burglary and property offenses generally, while the remaining parolees show a higher percentage of sex offenders, assault, narcotics violations, and homicide (the study groups have no such cases).

There are, then, some large differences between these two groups. A pertinent question, though, is the meaning of these differences. One cannot conclude from these data that the study group cases are at less risk of parole failure at 24 months than the remaining parolees. The two groups appear instead to be at least at equal risk of violating parole.

There are some hints, moreover, that the study cases may even be at greater risk of violating parole than the remaining parolees. For example, use of the exclusionary criteria increased the percentage of study group cases with commitment offenses against property—the largest category of offenders and those who, as a whole, run a high risk of failure. And even though the parolees other than the study group cases spent somewhat longer time in institutions before release to parole, there is no consistent relationship between length of stay in institutions and likelihood of parole violation for C.Y.A. parolees. (This is also true for parole outcomes at 24 months by race, Table A2-2.)

Another way to approach the question of comparability is to examine *actual* parole outcomes for the study group parolee cases and the remaining cases. These data are presented in Table A2-3 and indicate that there are no differences in discharge evaluation, percent discharged for whatever reason, and violation status at 15, 24, and 48 months.* There are, though, some differences

---

*Data taken from the July 1978 parole follow-up file, Information Systems Section, C.Y.A.

in the percent receiving mixed probation and jail sentences: 16 percent of the study groups and 8 percent of the remaining parolees received such sentences at off violation. Study group parolees were also more likely to receive jail sentences than the remaining parolees (21 percent versus 15 percent), and to receive jail sentences of one year or more (9 percent versus 5 percent). And a higher percentage of the parolees other than the study cases were likely to be discharged with no violation (52 percent versus 45 percent).

The implication of all this is that the parole performance of the parolees included in the study sample does not differ greatly—if at all—from that of the remaining parolees in the state. Differences in sentences may reflect variation in sentencing practices at the local level; they may also reflect the greater seriousness or extensity of law violation activity of the study group parolees. In any case the fundamental similarity of these two groups in this respect cannot be denied.

Table A2-2. Percentage of 1975 Parolees Violating Parole at 24 Months

Characteristics	Number Released	Number Violating	Percentage Violating
Race			
White	2,020	791	39.2
Mexican-American	886	366	41.3
Black	1,429	593	41.5
All others	123	51	41.5
Full Board/Special Service status			
Non-Full Board	2,806	1,154	41.1
Full Board or			
Full Board/Special Service	1,109	412	37.2
Special Service only	543	235	43.3
Felony-misdemeanor status			
Juvenile-21	2,275	1,075	47.2
Wobbler (Felony or			
Misdemeanor)	1,289	450	34.9
Misdemeanor	189	85	45.0
Felony	705	191	27.1
Admission status			
First commitment	2,964	1,109	37.4
Parole violators	1,494	692	46.3
New commitments	569	287	50.4
Parole returns	925	405	43.8

Table A2-3. Parole Follow-up Outcomes for Total Agency Population, Study Area Exclusions, and Study Groups

Follow-up Data	Total 12/31/75 Parolees No.	%	12/31/75 Parolees Less Exclusions No.	%	Exclusions No.	%	Study Group Parolees No.	%	Exclusions and Parolee Study Group No.	%
Reason for removal										
Discharged, no violation	3,801	52.2	3,621	52.7	180	43.9	90	45.4	270	44.4
No removal	460	6.3	437	6.4	23	5.6	17	8.6	40	6.6
No removal, serious violation	168	2.3	166	2.4	2	0.5	7	3.5	9	1.5
Recommitment	574	7.9	514	7.5	60	14.6	16	8.1	76	12.5
Revoked, no local sentence	280	3.8	268	3.9	12	2.9	5	2.5	17	2.8
Revoked, local sentence	120	1.6	114	1.6	6	1.5	4	2.0	10	1.6
15-month evaluation										
Violation	1,427	19.6	1,325	19.3	102	24.9	28	14.1	130	21.4
No violation	5,857	80.4	5,549	80.7	308	75.1	170	85.9	478	78.6
24-month evaluation										
Removed 24 month	1,665	22.9	1,547	22.5	118	28.8	38	19.2	156	25.6
Not removed	5,519	75.8	5,228	76.0	291	71.0	156	78.8	447	73.5
No information	100	1.4	99	1.4	1	0.2	4	2.0	5	0.8
48-month evaluation										
Removed 48 month	2,663	36.6	2,478	36.0	185	45.1	79	39.3	264	43.4
No removal	4,037	55.4	3,837	55.8	200	48.8	97	49.0	297	48.8
No information	584	8.0	559	8.1	25	6.1	22	11.0	47	7.7
Type violation at off violation										
Technical/other	32	0.4	30	0.4	2	0.5	1	0.5	3	0.5
Law violation, not prosecuted or guilty	43	0.6	43	0.6	0	0.0	0	0.0	0	0.0
Law prosecution pending, release to agency	414	5.7	381	5.5	33	8.0	14	7.1	47	7.7

Follow-up Data	No.	%	No.	%	No.	%	No.	%	No.	%
Type violation (continued)										
Probation	128	1.8	122	1.8	6	1.5	4	2.0	10	1.6
Jail	556	7.6	523	7.6	33	8.0	12	6.1	45	7.4
Probation and jail	559	7.7	526	7.6	33	8.0	31	15.7	64	10.5
Law: prison or agency	1,199	16.5	1,113	16.2	86	21.0	35	17.7	121	19.9
No action or AWOL	4,353	59.8	4,136	60.2	217	52.9	101	51.0	318	52.3
Jail sentence										
No jail	6,172	84.7	5,828	84.8	344	83.9	155	78.3	499	82.1
0-29 days	50	0.7	47	0.7	3	0.7	0	0.0	3	0.5
30-89 days	77	1.1	74	1.1	3	0.7	4	2.0	7	1.2
90-179 days	259	3.6	248	3.6	11	2.7	8	4.0	19	3.1
6-9 months	355	4.9	337	4.9	18	4.4	13	6.6	31	5.1
1 year +[a]	338	4.6	308	4.5	30	7.3	17	8.6	47	7.7
Jail 90 +	33	0.5	32	0.5	1	0.2	1	0.5	2	0.3
Total	7,284	100.0	6,874	100.0	410	100.0	198	100.0	608	100.0
Discharge evaluation										
None	1,602	22.0	1,499	21.8	103	25.1	48	24.2	151	24.8
Honorable	3,155	43.3	3,008	43.8	147	35.9	84	42.4	321	38.0
General	397	5.5	367	5.3	30	7.3	7	3.5	37	6.1
Dishonorable	2,130	29.2	2,000	29.1	130	31.7	59	29.8	189	31.1
Discharge status										
Not applicable	1,602	22.0	1,499	21.8	103	25.1	48	24.2	151	24.8
No violation	3,753	51.5	3,575	52.0	178	43.4	91	46.0	269	44.2
AWOL	407	5.6	380	5.5	27	6.6	4	2.0	31	5.1
Pending	408	5.6	375	5.4	33	8.0	14	7.1	47	7.7
Probation or jail	422	5.8	384	5.6	38	9.3	22	11.1	60	9.9
In-state prison	557	7.6	532	7.7	25	6.1	17	8.6	42	6.9
Federal or out-of-state prosecution	76	1.0	72	1.0	4	1.0	2	1.0	6	1.0
Death	1	a	1	a	0	a	0	a	0	a
Other	1	a	1	a	0	a	0	a	0	a

[a]Incompatible at conversion.

Appendix 3
The Course of
the Study

This study was a fluke. It was a fluke from the beginning.
—A Youth Authority Administrator

. . . It seems to be the eternal paradox of the human mind that
principles and faiths which are so essential to its comfort and to
the orderly organization and transmission of ideas should at the
same time always stand as the greatest obstacle to discovery.
—Thurman Arnold, *The Symbols of Government*

During a period of increasing aversion to research on prisoners, in obtaining access to records and in gaining cooperation to do research, it does not often occur that a study with random assignment makes it past the planning stages. Even when operation procedures have been developed for the purpose of random assignment they have in some cases been found to be subverted (University of Southern California, 1975).

The lack of randomization in studies on the effectiveness of parole, particularly in light of current proposals to abolish it, has been an impediment to undertaking studies on a grander scale. Part of the reason for this may lie in mistaken assumptions about the criminality of parolees released from prison (Greenburg, 1975, p. 556), methods of computing failure rates of parolees (Berecochea, et al., 1972), aside from organizational issues briefly alluded to in Chapter 1. Stanley's (1976, p. 3) observation, though, captures another extremely important aspect of the difficulty facing researchers who hope to implement experimental designs in parole research:

Parole boards and parole staff . . . work under a political spotlight.
They must please chief executives and legislators, compete success-
fully for funds, and demonstrate diligence and competence (if not
success) in working toward their goals. The spotlight is intense
because citizens are afraid of criminals who threaten violence or
invade their homes. When parole officials release an offender
who then commits a new crime, the social and political repercus-
sions are severe. Thus a major goal of parole boards and officials
becomes the avoidance of error—or at least of frightening, obvious,
publicized error.

Considerations such as these raise the question of how research experiments can ever be conducted. It would be useful, then, to learn how the present study came about and unfortunately never came to complete fruition.[1]

In January of 1974 a concept paper written by a parole manager named William C. (Bill) McCord appeared. It was entitled "The Differential Status Project," and provided a design and justification to study the effectiveness of three alternative release procedures: 1. direct discharge from institutions; 2. a voluntary services condition with no contacts or surveillance; contacts with the agent were to be instigated by the parolee. This condition was similar to that actualized in the Summary Parole Project (Star, 1979), noted earlier; and 3. regular parole supervision.

The project was developed into a proposal by McCord in May 1975, and presented to the Youth Authority Board in July and September of 1975. To obtain board approval McCord expanded the study area from one parole unit to three, in large part to increase the proportion of nonblacks in the study, and met with or talked to chief probation officers, chiefs of police, district attorneys, superior court judges, and others to assure their acceptance and explain the nature of the experiment. He also went to an institution in the C.Y.A. and spoke with wards in custody and solicited their opinions about the possibility of being discharged from parole and other issues. Eligibility criteria were developed for inclusion in the study. The parole board then approved the study in January 1976.

The eligibility criteria were then applied to the active caseloads in the three parole units by McCord and one other parole agent. A subsequent check of these procedures indicates that this work was done accurately.

A list of the parolees deemed eligible for random assignment was provided to the research division and wards were randomly assigned to one of the three experimental conditions. Letters of discharge were prepared and signed by one board member. An additional letter, displayed in Chapter 3, was composed by McCord and eventually sent along with the discharge order. These letters, along with those for wards assigned to the voluntary services condition, were signed in early February 1976, and placed in a briefcase pending final administrative approval of the project. Both Youth Authority legal counsel and McCord were aware of a board administrative rule which required that once an order of discharge was signed by a board member it was irrevocable.[2]

McCord, the then Director of the Youth Authority Allen Breed, parole agents in the field, and others eagerly anticipated the start of the project. The project had been supported by the board, although some conservative members were somewhat reticent. Even the governor's office had given it approval. To the surprise of most, if not all, the project was then "frozen" or suspended in a meeting which occurred in late February 1976. This event halted full implementation of the project as originally designed.

The reasons for the lack of full approval of the project are still a subject of gossip, rumor, and bitterness among those who expended a great deal of effort in getting it off the ground. Some argued that the project had requested too much in the way of extra positions, but others disagreed. It was pointed out that the agent-parolee ratio in the study area was below budget requirements and had been for some time, although to my knowledge no record of this argument exists. One further argument cynically suggested that the experiment itself was proposed to forestall the closing of a parole unit because of declining caseloads; one unit was in fact closed shortly after the project was scheduled to begin.

The most important reasons appear to lie elsewhere. At the same time the Differential Status Project was being considered the C.Y.A. was undergoing a parole reorganization which would have reduced the caseload sizes of agents and provided "enriched" services to parolees. Despite the fact that some Differential Status Project advocates felt that the project could serve as a built-in evaluation component of the parole reorganization plan, the Department of Finance did not. Breed, who stated that he supported the project, related in a telephone interview in December of 1979 that:

> The Department of Finance told us that they could not support
> our proposal to reduce the caseloads of parole agents statewide
> *if we went ahead with the project.* They told us that if we
> waited until the budget session of next year that they might
> be able to support it. I was faced with a difficult decision.
> Something had to happen. And at the last minute everything
> blew up.

The Department of Finance did interpret the project as needing extra positions. In the end—and ironically—the parole reorganization was not approved. Officially caseloads stood at 50:1 but were in face about 30:1 due to about 90 exempt positions. The parole reorganization was an attempt to have the 30:1 ratio approved.

An evaluation of Youth Authority parole by the Department of Finance, made at the request of the governor of the state, occurred during and shortly after preparation and termination of the project had occurred. One can glean from the study's conclusions that the Department of Finance did not strongly support a simple reduction in caseload size with a promise of reduction in recidivism. In fact, the report was clear in stating that C.Y.A. and other research had "not addressed the most fundamental questions. It is not yet known if the parole program and the parole agent can, or do, prevent criminal behavior." The Differential Status Project was viewed as a study which could provide "baseline data to support or refute" the assumption that parole prevents criminal behavior. The evaluators asserted that until such a study was conducted no "rigorous evaluation of the parole program" would be feasible.

Both the parole reorganization plan and the project held theoretically opposed, or at least challenging, assumptions about the efficacy of parole. The C.Y.A. may have been made to face up to study results which might find no differences in outcome between the three experimental groups. In the end, it appeared that the C.Y.A. would have been "damned if it did" or "damned if it didn't" endorse the Differential Status Project.

Given the suspension of the project the letters to the parolees assigned to the voluntary services condition were revoked. Those for the discharges, though, were mailed. As noted earlier, the procedure was followed in accordance with board policy and done with the cooperation of legal counsel in the C.Y.A. There were no parolee complaints.

For the sake of understanding it would be informative here to step back for a moment and place these events in a broader context. Due to the effects of probation subsidy in the decade preceding the study, commitments to the C.Y.A. dropped dramatically—as of 1975, first commitments had declined to 55 percent of what they had been in 1965. Increasingly individuals with more serious prior records and fewer individuals with first commitments from juvenile court entered the C.Y.A. The average age of the institutional and parole populations rose to a mean age of 20.4 years in 1976. Moreover, the mean length of stay on parole increased substantially during this decade (from 17.1 months in 1967 to 25.9 in 1974, declining to 21.5 in 1976).

The reasons for these changes, particularly the increase in length of stay on parole, are complex. In general, though, the increasing length of stay on parole has been associated with, if not due to a decline in commitments. This is not surprising and has not generated a great amount of attention.

The Differential Status Project, in turn, was proposed at a point in time when officials were precariously attempting to maintain existing (parole) field positions during a period of hiring freezes and austerity within state government generally. The reorganization was an attempt to adapt to this predicament. The Differential Status Project represented its antithesis: it questioned the predominant interpretation of the C.Y.A. mandate, which places great importance upon release to parole as a means of giving offenders an opportunity to demonstrate their ability to adapt to the community, made easier through the provision of services, counseling, and surveillance. How could a project which implicitly questioned the need for any supervision whatsoever compete with an incessant quest of most parole bureaucracies for the Holy Grail of parole—the ideal caseload size?

About a year after the project was frozen the remains of the study were exhumed and follow-up data for those discharged and one-half of those retained on parole (the originally assigned regular supervision cases) were collected for a 13-month period. The study was given a new title, the Bay Area Discharge (BAD) Project, and the acronym eventually summarized the status of the study and the reaction to the limited and preliminary follow-up (Jackson, 1978) in the eyes of a new director and a more conservative mood. The results of the study at best showed no difference between the two groups and at worse suggested the parolees were treated more punitively.

When released for in-house review the written reactions were either absent or negative: as with many reviews, some criticisms were quite good and raised important questions; others, however, missed the mark. For example:

1. There are a great many other ways to determine parole effectiveness. You *should* ask, "How does a parole system help the community?"
2. We don't need to hear this.
3. This is awful.
4. My opinion of the report is that all copies should be quickly gathered up and run through the paper shredder. (This statement was later withdrawn but not without a reprimand.)
5. The parole services provided the cases discharged from parole prior to discharge might have reduced their violational behavior after discharge.

More sympathetic criticisms pointed out that further data analysis needed to be done, that arrest data were not adequate follow-up measures, that there were too few cases for meaningful policy change, that the time period of the follow-up was too short, and that the study groups might not be comparable to all parolees in the agency at the time of the study.

Some (but not all) of these criticisms were taken up in the 13 revisions the study went through before being publicly distributed. Although the original data did not, of course, change, the conclusion of the preliminary study was nonetheless that, at best, there were no systematic differences between the two groups. The name of the study was changed to "defuse" the political atmosphere. The parole reorganization plan proposed to the Department of Finance was eventually given at least partial approval during the period of these revisions; the delay may have had some bearing on getting the proposal approved. The then governor's office requested a copy of the study before it was approved by the executive team, the highest level of review in the C.Y.A., although nothing became of this other than the then governor's comment, paraphrased, to C.Y.A. administrators: "I know parole does not reduce crime but my constituency wants it."

In sum, the project became defined by some in the C.Y.A. as one which should not have occurred and which probably should not be granted wide support as an ongoing experimental project. Evidence for this view is shown in the response of the C.Y.A. to the Department of Finance report claiming that no study exists to show that parole prevents criminality and that the Differential Status Project could provide such "baseline data."[3] The official response to this point was that:

Carefully designed experimental programs should be implemented and evaluated [but] experimental programs are expensive and *we*

> *cannot finance them by reduction of services designed to provide*
> *protection to the public.* [emphasis supplied]

Presumably this included parole services.

The message was also brought home to line agents in the study area after the suspension of the project by a newly appointed parole division head. Some agents expressed the view that it was a "time to test basic principles" of parole. The reply, putting the agents firmly in their place, was that, "You might be courageous, but it [the study] might be a determinant of jobs."

In the meantime, as Allen Breed points out, the project approval by the board was never rescinded; it "is still in a holding pattern and something could conceivably come of it." Indeed, given the finding of the present study that parole supervision has no effects or negative effects—thereby removing preliminary fears of "risk to the public" due to the lack of supervision—the times appear more propitious for a larger-scale study in line with the original proposal. Whether this comes into being remains to be seen.

NOTES

1. A previous version of this paper was presented at the Association for Criminal Justice Research Meetings, Claremont, California, May 1979.

2. Of course it was not inevitable that the letters should be mailed. The thought of not mailing them could have been entertained. The board member who signed them was later anxious about learning the study results. Given the study findings that homicide and rape charges and convictions were concentrated among the parolees retained on parole, these fears should be somewhat abated.

When this researcher asked one high-level administrator in the Department of Corrections why the Summary Parole Project, which had originally included a discharge component in planning stages, was not eventually implemented, his only remark was: "We're better politicians." (Statement made at the Association for Criminal Justice Research [California] Meetings, May 1979.)

3. The irony of this is that the Department of Finance was largely responsible for the demise of the Differential Status Project.

Appendix 4
Severity of
Offense Categories

Severity Code	Offense
9	Murder
	Manslaughter (except vehicular)
	Attempted murder; assault with intent to kill
8	Assault with a deadly weapon
	Armed robbery
	Forcible sex acts
7	Strongarm robbery
	Pursesnatching
	Burglary; attempted burglary
	Grand theft; larceny
	Auto theft
	Arson
6	Battery on a peace officer (resisting arrest)
	Assault; battery
	Child abuse
	Extortion
	Other offenses against persons (threats, etc.)
	Burglary, auto; auto tampering
5	Joyriding
	Vandalism; destruction of property
	Breaking and entering
	Forgery, bad checks, credit cards
	Weapons: display, possession, discharging firearms
	Receiving or possession of stolen property
	Other property offenses (fraud)
	Selling or furnishing narcotics or drugs
4	Sex offenses without force; sex perversion; indecent exposure
	Prostitution; soliciting
	Lewd acts on a child; molesting
	Other sex offenses
	Malicious mischief
	Petty theft
3	Possession, use of or under the influence of drugs or narcotics
	Selling or furnishing marijuana
	Marijuana; possession, use, under influence, cultivating, possession of paraphenalia, etc.
	Traffic: Vehicular manslaughter

Severity Code	Offense
3 (continued)	Traffic: Hit and run
	Traffic: Drunk driving
	Facility escape; AWOL
	Statutory rape
2	Drunk; drinking problem; possession of alcohol
	Glue sniffing
	Disturbing the peace
	Disorderly conduct; fighting
	Trespassing
	Traffic: Reckless driving
	Other antisocial acts which could result in an arrest (such as violation of probation or a court order)
1	Beyond control; incorrigible
	Runaway (home, fosterhome, or camp)
	Truancy
	Foster home failure
	Curfew
	Other noncriminal offenses (such as loitering)
	Traffic citations
0	Protective custody
	Neglected child
	Molested child

Appendix 5
Disposition Code

Code	Disposition
01	Warrants, disposition unknown
02	Don't know if charged or convicted, no information (excludes warrants)
03	Charges not yet filed, warrant outstanding
04	Escaped, returned to commitment without charging
05	Investigative arrest only, released
06	849 (b) (1)—released, deemed not an arrest
07	Released by police other than 849 (b)
08	Released to juvenile authorities or petition requested, no further information
09	Charges filed, but: off-calendar, certified to juvenile court, insane at commission, insane pending trial, warrant outstanding
10	Dismissed at intake
11	Informal probation by probation intake
12	Case dismissed or discharged at court (UNLESS 13)
13	Case dismissed or "disappeared" at the same time other charge(s) were sustained
14	Acquitted
15	Convicted, don't know sentence
16	Fine $0-99
17	Fine $100-199
18	Fine $200-299
19	Fine $300+
20	Choice of fine or jail, choice unspecified
21	Formal probation without wardship
22	Formal probation with wardship (CODE 21 IF UNCERTAIN)
23	Jail (1-29)
24	Jail (30-179)
25	Jail (180 or more)
26	County-level boys facility commitment (boys ranch, senior boys camp, 24-hour boarding school, etc.)
27	Mental hospital commitment
28	California Rehabilitation Center (C.R.C.) commitment
29	California Youth Authority (C.Y.A.) commitment
30	California Department of Corrections (C.D.C.) commitment
31	No actual sentence—everything suspended
32	OTHER (SPECIFY)_____

Note: The highest numbered code took precedence. If there was a combination of dispositions, the most serious one was coded. Jail was most serious, probation next, and fine least serious.

Bibliography

Adams, William P., Paul M. Chandler, and M.G. Neithercutt. "The San Francisco Project: A Critique." *Federal Probation* 35: 45-53, 1971.

Ageton, S. and D. Elliott. "The Effects of Legal Processing on Delinquent Orientations." *Social Problems* 22: 87-100, 1974.

Arnold, Thurman. *The Symbols of Government.* New Haven, Connecticut: Yale University Press, 1935.

Banks, Jerry, Terry Siler, and Ronald L. Rardin. "Past and Present Findings in Intensive Adult Probation." *Federal Probation* 41: 20-25, 1977.

Battaglia, C. "Deviant Behavior of Parolees and the Decision-Making Process of Parole Supervisors." Unpublishéd Ph.D. dissertation, Florida State University, 1968.

Bennett, L. and M. Zeigler. "Early Discharge: A Suggested Approach to Increased Efficiency in Parole." *Federal Probation* 39: 27-30, 1975.

Berecochea, John, Alfred N. Himelson, and Donald E. Miller. "The Risk of Failure During the Early Parole Period: A Methodological Note." *Journal of Criminal Law, Criminology and Police Science* 63: 93-97, 1972.

Bolen, Jane K. "The California Youth Authority: 1941-1971. Structure, Policies and Practices." Unpublished Ph.D. dissertation, University of Southern California, 1972.

Bottomley, A. Keith. *Decisions in the Penal Process.* South Hackensack, New Jersey: Fred B. Rothman, 1973.

Boulding, Kenneth E. *The Impact of the Social Sciences.* New Brunswick, New Jersey: Rutgers University Press, 1966.

Braly, Malcolm. *False Starts.* Boston: Little, Brown, 1976.

Bunker, Edward. *No Beast So Fierce.* New York: W. W. Norton, 1973.

Burkhart, Walter R. "The Great California Parole Experiment." *Federal Probation* 40: 9-26, 1976.

California Department of the Youth Authority. *Parole Services Administrative Manual.*

_____. *1978 Annual Plan.* Mimeographed, 1978.

California Rules of Court. *West's California Rules of Court.* St. Paul, Minnesota: West, 1977.

Chambliss, William J. "Types of Deviance and the Effectiveness of Legal Sanctions." *Wisconsin Law Review* 1967: 703-719, 1967.

Citizen's Inquiry on Parole and Criminal Justice, Inc. *Prison Without Walls: Report on New York Parole.* New York: Praeger, 1975.

Cook, Thomas D. and Donald T. Campbell. *Quasi-Experimentation: Design and Analysis Issues for Field Settings.* Chicago: Rand McNally College, 1979.

Davies, Martin. *Prisoners of Society.* London: Routledge and Kegan Paul, 1974.

Davis, Carolyn. "1975 Parole Agent Time Study." Sacramento, California Department of the Youth Authority. Mimeographed, 1975.

Department of Offender Rehabilitation. "A Study of Recommitment Rates for Inmates Released from Custody during Calendar Years 1973 and 1974." Bureau of Planning, Research and Statistics, Florida. Mimeographed, 1977.

Dembo, Richard. "Orientation and Activities of the Parole Officer." *Criminology* 10: 193-215, 1972.

Emerson, Robert M. *Judging Delinquents: Context and Process in Juvenile Court.* Chicago: Aldine, 1969.

Fogel, David. ". . . *We Are the Living Proof* . . ." Cincinnati: W. H. Anderson, 1975.

Foote, Caleb. "The Sentencing Function." In *Chief Justice Earl Warren Conference in the United States, A Program for Prison Reform*, pp. 7-19. Cambridge, Mass.: Roscoe Pound American Trial Lawyers Foundation, 1973.

Gibbs, J. P. *Crime, Punishment, and Deterrence.* New York: Elsevier, 1975.

Glaser, Daniel. *Effectiveness of a Prison and Parole System.* Indianapolis: Bobbs-Merrill, 1964.

_____. *Social Deviance.* Chicago: Markham, 1971.

_____. *Routinizing Evaluation: Getting Feedback on Effectiveness of Crime and Delinquency Programs.* Washington, D.C.: National Institute of Mental Health, Center for Studies of Crime and Delinquency, 1973.

Goodman, John L. "Is Ordinary Least Squares Estimation with a Dichotomous Dependent Variable Really That Bad?" Washington, D.C.: The Urban Institute, 1975.

Gottesman, Michael and Lewis J. Hecker. "Parole: A Critique of Legal Foundations and Conditions." *New York University Law Review* 38: 702-739, 1963.

Gottfredson, M.R., S. D. Mitchell-Herzfeld, and T. J. Flanagan. "Another Look at the Effectiveness of Parole Supervision." *Journal of Research in Crime and Delinquency* 19: 277-298, 1982.

Greenburg, David F. "The Incapacitative Effect of Imprisonment: Some Estimates." *Law and Society Review* 9: 541-580, 1975.

_____. "The Correctional Effects of Corrections: A Survey of Evaluations." In *Corrections and Punishment*, edited by David F. Greenburg, pp. 111-148. Beverly Hills, California: Sage, 1977.

Heaton, Wanda S. and Stuart Adams. "Community Performance of Three Categories of Institutional Releasees." Research Report No. 15. District of Columbia Department of Corrections, 1969.

Henry, A. F. and J. F. Short. *Suicide and Homicide.* New York: Free Press, 1954.

Herz, John H. "Legitimacy: Can We Retrieve It?" *Comparative Politics* 10: 317-343, 1978.

Hudson, C. "An Experimental Study of the Differential Effects of Parole Supervision for a Group of Adolescent Boys and Girls: A Summary. Minneapolis Department of Corrections, 1972.

Irwin, John. *The Felon.* Englewood Cliffs, New Jersey: Prentice-Hall, 1970.

Jackson, Patrick G. "Living Together Unmarried: Awareness Contexts and Social Interaction." *Journal of Family Issues* (forthcoming), 1983.

_____. "Bay Area Parole Project." California Department of the Youth Authority. Mimeographed, 1978.

_____. "Some Effects of Parole Supervision on Recidivism." *British Journal of Criminology* 23 (January), 1983.

Jaman, D., L. Bennett, and J. Berecochea. *Early Discharge from Parole: Policy, Practice and Outcome.* Research Report No. 51. Sacramento: California Department of Corrections, 1974.

Jensen, G. F. "Delinquency and Adolescent Self-Conception: A Study of the Personal Relevance of Infraction." *Social Problems* 20: 84-103, 1972.

Judd, C. M. and D. A. Kenny. *Estimating the Effects of Social Interventions.* New York: Cambridge University Press, 1981.

Kassebaum, Gene, David A. Ward, and Daniel M. Wilner. *Prison Treatment and Parole Survival.* New York: John Wiley, 1971.

Kitsuse, J. I. and A. Cicourel. "A Note on the Uses of Official Statistics." *Social Problems* 11: 131-139, 1963.

Lemert, Edwin M. *Human Deviance, Social Problems, and Social Control.* Englewood Cliffs, New Jersey: Prentice-Hall, 1972.

Lerman, Paul. *Community Treatment and Social Control.* Chicago: University of Chicago Press, 1972.

Lerner, Mark Jay. "The Effectiveness of a Definite Sentence Parole Program." *Criminology* 15: 211-224, 1977.

Lipton, Douglas, Robert Martinson, and Judith Wilks. *The Effectiveness of Correctional Treatment.* New York: Praeger, 1975.

McArthur, A. Verne. *Coming Out Cold.* Lexington: 1974.

McCleary, Richard. *Dangerous Men: The Sociology of Parole.* Beverly Hills: California: Sage, 1978.

McGee, Richard A. "A New Look at Sentencing: Part II." *Federal Probation* 38: 3-11, 1974.

Manning, Peter K. *Police Work: The Social Organization of Policing.* Cambridge: The MIT Press, 1977.

Martinson, Robert M., Gene G. Kassebaum, and David A. Ward. "A Critique of Research in Parole." In *Probation and Parole: Selected Readings,* edited by Robert M. Carter and Leslie T. Wilkins, pp. 643-650. New York: Wiley, 1970.

Martinson, Robert and Judith Wilks. "Save Parole Supervision." *Federal Probation* 41: 23-27, 1977.

Mead, G. "The Psychology of Punitive Justice." *American Sociological Review* 23: 577-602, 1928.

Messinger, Sheldon. "Strategies of Control." Unpublished Ph.D. dissertation, Center for the Study of Law and Society, University of California at Berkeley, 1969.

_____. "Introduction. In *The Question of Parole*, edited by Andrew von Hirsch and Kathleen J. Hanrahan. Cambridge, Massachusetts: Ballinger, 1979.

Minor, W. William and Michael Courlander. "The Postrelease Trauma Thesis: A Reconsideration of the Risk of Early Parole Failure." *Journal of Research in Crime and Delinquency* 16: 273-293, 1979.

Morris, Norval. *The Habitual Offender*. Cambridge, Massachusetts: Harvard University Press, 1951.

Morris, Pauline and Farida Beverly. *On License: A Study of Parole*. New York: Wiley, 1975.

Moseley, W. H. "Parole: How It Is Working." *Journal of Criminal Justice* 5: 185-203, 1977.

Neithercutt, M. G. "Parole Violation Patterns and Commitment Offenses." *Journal of Research in Crime and Delinquency* 9: 87-98, 1972.

_____ and D. M. Gottfredson. "Caseload Size Variation and Difference in Probation/Parole Performance." Paper prepared for the Federal Judicial Center, Washington, D.C., 1973.

National Advisory Commission on Criminal Justice Standards and Goals. *Corrections*. Washington, D.C.: U.S. Government Printing Office, 1973.

Ohlin, Lloyd. *Sociology and the Field of Corrections*. New York: Russell Sage Foundation, 1956.

O'Leary, Vincent. "Parole Theory and Outcomes Reexamined." *Criminal Law Bulletin* 11: 304-317, 1975.

_____ and Kathleen Hanrahan. "Law and Practice in Parole Proceedings: A National Survey." *Criminal Law Bulletin* 13: 181-211, 1977.

Orland, Leonard. *Prisons: Houses of Darkness.* New York: Free Press, 1975.

Palmer, Ted. "The Youth Authority's Community Treatment Project." *Federal Probation* 38: 3-14, 1974.

Parker, William. *Parole: Origins, Development, Current Practices, and Statutes.* American Correctional Association, Parole Corrections Project, Resource Document No. 1, College Park, Maryland: American Correctional Association, 1975.

Petersilia, Joan, Peter W. Greenwood, and Marvin Lavin. *Criminal Careers of Habitual Felons.* Santa Monica: Rand, 1977.

Robinson, Paul.H. "Parole Holds: Their Effect on the Rights of the Parolee and the Operation of the Parole System." *UCLA Law Review* 19: 759-803, 1972.

Robison, J. and Gerald Smith. "The Effectiveness of Correctional Programs." *Crime and Delinquency* 17: 67-80, 1971.

_____ and Paul Takagi. "The Parole Violator as an Organization Reject." In *Probation and Parole: Selected Readings*, edited by R. Carter and L. Wilkins, pp. 233-254. New York: Wiley, 1970.

Robison, J. O., L. T. Wilkins, R. M. Carter, and A. Awhl. *The San Francisco Project.* School of Criminology, Berkeley: University of California, 1969.

Rossi, Peter H., Emily Waite, Christine E. Bose, and Richard Berk. "The Seriousness of Crimes: Normative Structure and Individual Differences." *American Sociological Review* 39: 224-237, 1974.

Rubin, Sol. "New Sentencing Proposals and Laws in the 1970's." *Federal Probation* 43: 3-8, 1979.

Sacks, Howard R. and Charles H. Logan. *Does Parole Make a Difference?* University of Connecticut School of Law Press, 1979.

Schwartz, Richard D. and Jerome H. Skolnick. "Two Studies of Legal Stigma." In *Society and the Legal Order*, edited by Richard D. Schwartz and Jerome H. Skolnick, pp. 566-574. New York: Basic Books, 1970.

Sellin, T and M. Wolfgang. *The Measurement of Delinquency.* New York: Wiley, 1964.

Sheehan, Susan. "Annals of Crime, Part III." *The New Yorker*, November 7, 1977, pp. 133-202, 1977.

Sigler, Maurice. "Abolish Parole? " *Federal Probation* 39: 42-48, 1975.

Silberman, Matthew. "Toward a Theory of Criminal Deterrence." *American Sociological Review* 41: 442-461, 1976.

Smith, Robert Lee. "Youth and Correction: An Institutional Analysis of the California Youth Authority." Unpublished M.A. thesis, University of California, 1949.

Stanley, David T. *Prisoners Among Us: The Problem of Parole.* Washington, D.C.: The Brookings Institution, 1976.

Star, Deborah. *Summary Parole: A Six and Twelve Month Follow-up Evaluation.* Research Report No. 60. California Department of Corrections, 1979.

_____ and John E. Berecochea. *Rationalizing the Conditions of Parole: Some Recommended Changes.* Research Report No. 58. California Department of Corrections, 1977.

_____, John E. Berecochea, and David Petrocchi. *Return to Prison Ordered: Policy in Practice and Change.* Sacramento: California Department of Corrections, unpublished manuscript, 1978.

State of California, Department of Finance. "California Youth Authority Parole Program Effectiveness (October)." Mimeographed, 1976.

Studt, Elliot. "The Reentry of the Offender into the Community." U.S. Department of Health, Education and Welfare, 1967.

_____. *Surveillance and Service in Parole.* Washington, D.C.: U.S. Department of Justice, Law Enforcement Assistance Administration, National Institute of Law Enforcement and Criminal Justice, 1973.

Takagi, Paul. "Evaluation and Adaptations in a Formal Organization." Unpublished Ph.D. dissertation, Stanford University, 1967.

Thomas, Wayne H. *Bail Reform in America.* University of California Press, 1976.

Thornberry, T.P. "Punishment and Crime: The Effect of Legal Dispositions on Subsequent Criminal Behavior." Unpublished Ph.D. dissertation, University of Philadelphia, 1971.

Tittle, Charles R. "Deterrents or Labeling?" *Social Forces* 53: 399-410, 1975.

Twentieth Century Task Fund. *Confronting Youth Crime. Report of the Twentieth Century Fund Task Force on Sentencing Policy Toward Young Offenders.* New York: Holmes and Meier, 1978.

University of Southern California. "Alternative Dispositions for Juvenile Offenders." Social Science Research Institute. Mimeographed, 1975.

United States Department of Justice. *The Attorney General's Survey of Release Procedures: Parole, Volume 4.* Washington, D.C.: U.S. Government Printing Office, 1939.

von Hirsch, Andrew and Katheryn Hanrahan. *Abolish Parole?* National Institute of Law Enforcement and Criminal Justice, Law Enforcement Assistance Administration, U.S. Department of Justice. Republished as: *The Question of Parole: Retention, Reform, or Abolition?* Cambridge, Massachusetts: Ballinger, 1978.

Waldo, Gordon P. and Theodore G. Chiricos. "Perceived Penal Sanction and Self-reported Criminology: A Neglected Approach to Deterrence Research." *Social Problems* 19: 522-540, 1972.

Waller, Irvin. "Parole for the Ex-Prisoner: Carrot, Stick or Illusion?" In *The Future of Parole*, edited by D. J. West, pp. 116-134. London: Duckworth, 1972.

_____. *Men Released from Prison.* University of Toronto Press, 1974.

West, D. J. *The Future of Parole.* London: Duckworth, 1972.

Yankelovich, Daniel. "A Crisis of Moral Legitimacy?" *Dissent* 21: 526-533, 1974.

Zimring, Franklin E. and Gordon J. Hawkins. "Deterrence and Marginal Groups." *Journal of Research in Crime and Delinquency* 5: 100-114, 1968.

_____. *Deterrence.* Chicago: University of Chicago Press, 1973.

Zuckerman, Stanley B., Alfred J. Barron, and Horace B. Whittier. "A Follow-up Study of Minnesota State Reformatory Inmates: A Preliminary Report." *Journal of Criminal Law, Criminology and Police Science* 43: 622-636, 1952.

Zumbrun, Alvin and John Berry. "A Follow-up Study of Men Released in 1954 from the State Reformatory for Males, by Reason of Parole and Expiration of Sentence." Final Report. Baltimore, Criminal Justice Commission, mimeographed, June 1958.

Index

About the Author

PATRICK G. JACKSON is a Professor of Sociology at the University of California, Davis. He is also a Senior Associate at the National Council on Crime and Delinquency, San Francisco, and a research fellow at the University of California Davis Law School.

Dr. Jackson has published both in the United States and abroad. His articles have appeared in the *British Journal of Criminology* and *Journal of Family Issues* and through various governmental agencies. His forthcoming work on methods in criminology will be published through the University of Rome.

Dr. Jackson holds a B.A. from California State University, Fresno, and an M.A. and Ph.D. from the University of California, Davis.